NATIONAL ACADEMIES Sciences Engineering Medicine

NATIONAL ACADEMIES PRESS
Washington, DC

Implications of Artificial Intelligence–Related Data Center Electricity Use and Emissions

Convened November 12–13, 2024

Anne Frances Johnson and
Kasia Kornecki, *Rapporteurs*

Roundtable on Artificial Intelligence
and Climate Change

Board on Energy and
Environmental Systems

Division on Engineering and
Physical Sciences

Proceedings of a Workshop

NATIONAL ACADEMIES PRESS 500 Fifth Street, NW Washington, DC 20001

This activity was supported by Google, the Heising-Simon Foundation, IBM, Microsoft, the Patrick J. McGovern Foundation, the William and Floral Hewlett Foundation, and a grant from the Chan Zuckerberg Initiative DAF, an advised fund of the Silicon Valley Community Foundation. Any opinions, findings, conclusions, or recommendations expressed in this publication do not necessarily reflect the views of any organization or agency that provided support for the project.

International Standard Book Number-13: 978-0-309-99204-6
Digital Object Identifier: https://doi.org/10.17226/29101

This publication is available from the National Academies Press, 500 Fifth Street, NW, Keck 360, Washington, DC 20001; (800) 624-6242; https://nap.nationalacademies.org.

The manufacturer's authorized representative in the European Union for product safety is Authorised Rep Compliance Ltd., Ground Floor, 71 Lower Baggot Street, Dublin D02 P593 Ireland; www.arccompliance.com.

Printed in the United States of America.

Suggested citation: National Academies of Sciences, Engineering, and Medicine. 2025. *Implications of Artificial Intelligence–Related Data Center Electricity Use and Emissions: Proceedings of a Workshop*. Washington, DC: National Academies Press. https://doi.org/10.17226/29101.

The **National Academy of Sciences** was established in 1863 by an Act of Congress, signed by President Lincoln, as a private, nongovernmental institution to advise the nation on issues related to science and technology. Members are elected by their peers for outstanding contributions to research. Dr. Marcia McNutt is president.

The **National Academy of Engineering** was established in 1964 under the charter of the National Academy of Sciences to bring the practices of engineering to advising the nation. Members are elected by their peers for extraordinary contributions to engineering. Dr. John L. Anderson is president.

The **National Academy of Medicine** (formerly the Institute of Medicine) was established in 1970 under the charter of the National Academy of Sciences to advise the nation on medical and health issues. Members are elected by their peers for distinguished contributions to medicine and health. Dr. Victor J. Dzau is president.

The three Academies work together as the **National Academies of Sciences, Engineering, and Medicine** to provide independent, objective analysis and advice to the nation and conduct other activities to solve complex problems and inform public policy decisions. The National Academies also encourage education and research, recognize outstanding contributions to knowledge, and increase public understanding in matters of science, engineering, and medicine.

Learn more about the National Academies of Sciences, Engineering, and Medicine at **www.nationalacademies.org**.

Consensus Study Reports published by the National Academies of Sciences, Engineering, and Medicine document the evidence-based consensus on the study's statement of task by an authoring committee of experts. Reports typically include findings, conclusions, and recommendations based on information gathered by the committee and the committee's deliberations. Each report has been subjected to a rigorous and independent peer-review process and it represents the position of the National Academies on the statement of task.

Proceedings published by the National Academies of Sciences, Engineering, and Medicine chronicle the presentations and discussions at a workshop, symposium, or other event convened by the National Academies. The statements and opinions contained in proceedings are those of the participants and are not endorsed by other participants, the planning committee, or the National Academies.

Rapid Expert Consultations published by the National Academies of Sciences, Engineering, and Medicine are authored by subject-matter experts on narrowly focused topics that can be supported by a body of evidence. The discussions contained in rapid expert consultations are considered those of the authors and do not contain policy recommendations. Rapid expert consultations are reviewed by the institution before release.

For information about other products and activities of the National Academies, please visit www.nationalacademies.org/about/whatwedo.

PLANNING COMMITTEE FOR IMPLICATIONS OF ARTIFICIAL INTELLIGENCE–RELATED DATA CENTER ELECTRICITY USE AND EMISSIONS: A WORKSHOP

BENJAMIN C. LEE, University of Pennsylvania, *Chair*
AYSE COSKUN, Boston University
BENJAMIN KROPOSKI, Power Systems Engineering Center, National Renewable Energy Laboratory
ERIC MASANET, University of California, Santa Barbara
PRASHANT SHENOY, University of Massachusetts Amherst
CAROLE-JEAN WU, Meta

Staff

KASIA KORNECKI, Senior Program Officer
JASMINE VICTORIA BRYANT, Research Associate
NNEKA UDEAGBALA, Associate Program Officer
K. JOHN HOLMES, Senior Board Director/Scholar

Reviewers

This Proceedings of a Workshop was reviewed in draft form by individuals chosen for their diverse perspectives and technical expertise. The purpose of this independent review is to provide candid and critical comments that will assist the National Academies of Sciences, Engineering, and Medicine in making each published proceedings as sound as possible and to ensure that it meets the institutional standards for quality, objectivity, evidence, and responsiveness to the charge. The review comments and draft manuscript remain confidential to protect the integrity of the process.

We thank the following individuals for their review of this proceedings:

TANYA DAS, Bipartisan Policy Center
GEORGE KAMIYA, GSMA External Affairs
TAMARA KNEESE, Data and Society Research Institute

Although the reviewers listed above provided many constructive comments and suggestions, they were not asked to endorse the content of the proceedings nor did they see the final draft before its release. The review of this proceedings was overseen by **JUAN MORENO-CRUZ,** University of Waterloo. He was responsible for making certain that an independent examination of this proceedings was carried out in accordance with the standards of the National Academies and that all review comments were carefully considered. Responsibility for the final content rests entirely with the rapporteurs and the National Academies.

Contents

APPENDIXES

Overview

In recent years, the global adoption of artificial intelligence (AI) has spurred significant construction and investment in new data centers and cloud computing. These data centers require large-scale continuous power, posing challenges for local electric grids and broader climate goals. To explore how to map, measure, and mitigate the impacts of AI data center electricity usage, the National Academies of Sciences, Engineering, and Medicine convened the workshop Implications of Artificial Intelligence–Related Data Center Electricity Use and Emissions in Washington, DC, on November 12–13, 2024. Organized through the National Academies' Roundtable on Artificial Intelligence and Climate Change, the event gathered more than 95 in-person and more than 350 virtual participants from academia, the technology industry, electric utilities, community advocacy groups, and government agencies to discuss how recent AI developments could impact energy demands, identify options to mitigate increased electricity use and emissions, and consider regional implications related to data center siting and renewable resource availability.

The workshop aimed to foster shared learning and enhanced coordination as stakeholders work to understand and mitigate the technical, social, behavioral, and environmental impacts of AI data centers and their unique energy needs, with a focus on how these issues are unfolding in the United States. Attendees considered the available evidence on current and future trends in AI adoption, discussed technical and policy solutions that could help to mitigate AI data centers' large energy demands and their associated carbon emissions and impacts on local communities, and identified data and modeling gaps and needs relevant to improving understanding of these issues. They also discussed how AI technologies can potentially be leveraged to improve the grid and accelerate decarbonization goals by facilitating efficiency improvements both in data centers and across the economy more broadly. In presentations and moderated discussions, speakers examined the projected power demands from proposed new data centers and implications for the grid, sustainability goals, and local economies and communities and discussed challenges and opportunities in data center infrastructure and hardware–software interactions that could influence the efficiency of AI data centers in the future.

Over the course of the workshop, participants gained a new understanding of the scope and scale of the issues, as well as insights into potential solutions, knowledge and research gaps, and opportunities to create interdisciplinary, collaborative teams to advance innovation in this space. In the workshop's final session, members of the planning committee reflected on key issues that emerged from the discussions and contributed their thoughts on knowledge gaps and future directions for research, policy, and innovation.

TRENDS IN ARTIFICIAL INTELLIGENCE USE AND RELATED DATA CENTER ENERGY DEMANDS

Throughout the workshop, invited experts shared information on past and current energy demands for AI, particularly in data centers, along with projections for the future. Several speakers highlighted how technological advancements have led to tremendous gains in AI system performance and efficiency over the past decade, but described how gains in energy efficiency have been outpaced by the rapid growth in computing demands and data center expansions. This has resulted in a net increase in energy demands from AI data centers that is projected to accelerate further in the coming years. Much of the growth in data center infrastructure is concentrated in specific regions (e.g., Northern Virginia) due to factors such as fiber optic network availability, business-friendly policies and incentives, affordable power and water, and a skilled workforce. However, this regional clustering can create uneven impacts on local electric power grids and communities across the United States and globally.

Yet, the uncertainty in data center–driven load growth is high—some analyses suggest that energy use by AI workloads is overestimated, and some high-end projections suggest usage could double or even triple by 2030. To put this in perspective, in 2023, data centers accounted for

4.4 percent of total U.S. electricity consumption[1]—a relatively small share compared to other sources—and AI represents only a portion of activity within data centers. The expansion of AI data centers is also unfolding alongside broader trends in electrification and decarbonization, and overall electricity demand is rising as electrification accelerates across other industries such as transportation, manufacturing, and buildings, adding to the uncertainty in demand projections.

The real challenge and opportunity is the speed at which data centers require additional power, which could serve as a catalyst for accelerating grid modernization and advancing beneficial electrification across other sectors. This speed, however, amplifies the challenges that electric power utilities and grid operators face in keeping pace with rising demand—and avoiding the pitfalls of either overbuilding or underbuilding infrastructure—while striving to meet decarbonization goals by increasing clean energy generation and reducing fossil fuel use. Several speakers described how utilities have used projected increases in energy demands from AI data centers as justification for delaying the retirement of fossil fuel generation plants, or bringing new gas generators online, posing a setback for meeting decarbonization targets. This is compounded by the fact that utilities are typically incentivized to prioritize the cheapest and most reliable sources of electricity—often natural gas—rather than those with the lowest carbon emissions.

Despite the challenges related to grid generation capacity, several speakers pointed out that the availability of AI tools and the expansion of AI data centers also present new opportunities to modernize the electric grid and support greater efficiency and reliability. For example, if the electricity demands of data centers can be more flexible, more of their energy needs can be met through renewable generation; in addition, various demand response and market participation arrangements can position data centers as a partner to utilities in helping to increase grid capacity and ensure reliability.

While use of AI is growing and driving new investments in infrastructure, it currently represents only a portion of the total activity within data centers. Most data centers still primarily support a wide range of non-AI workloads, such as cloud computing, web hosting, and storage. As a result, the societal impacts of AI—such as changes in labor, education, and decision-making—are distinct from the broader environmental and energy impacts associated with data centers. It is challenging but important to separate these conversations: AI's influence on society will

[1] A. Shehabi, S.J. Smith, A. Hubbard, et al., 2024, *2024 United States Data Center Energy Usage Report*, LBNL-2001637, Lawrence Berkeley National Laboratory, https://eta-publications.lbl.gov/sites/default/files/2024-12/lbnl-2024-united-states-data-center-energy-usage-report.pdf.

depend on how extensively it is used and how efficient models become, while the operational footprint of data centers stems from their overall workload mix, infrastructure design, and energy practices.

Workshop planning committee chair Benjamin C. Lee, University of Pennsylvania, highlighted several points raised around trends and future use cases for large language models (LLMs). For example, AI algorithms can be redesigned to require fewer operations and less data movement, with the potential to create 10–100-fold improvements in efficiency. Designing more domain-specific and specialized machine learning models to use in place of larger, general models can also potentially drive discoveries in medicine, science, and business at much lower computational costs, although the energy efficiency implications of this approach are as yet unknown.

Despite all the opportunities around flexibility and efficiency, several speakers suggested that improving efficiency is not likely to be a major focus for AI developers until and unless LLMs become monetized. Until then, financial and regulatory incentives may be required for companies to design technologies in ways that are less energy intensive—the cost of electricity is trivial in comparison to capital expenditures on hardware.

Another consideration relevant to the future use of AI and associated energy demand is the degree to which users will tolerate latency, or the length of time it takes for data to travel between the user and the server and back. Factors such as proximity to Internet Exchange Points, high-density fiber optic networks, and direct cloud connections all affect latency, making data center location a crucial consideration. As a result, edge computing is becoming more popular to reduce delays. Beyond user experience, longer latencies can also pose security risks, as data rerouted through multiple locations become vulnerable to interception. Both latency tolerance and throughput (the number of responses an AI can generate per second) influence AI model design and energy efficiency. However, several speakers noted that it is still unclear how much latency users will accept, given the early stage of LLM deployment.

Multimodal models, which process text alongside images, audio, and video, present another potential complexity for energy demand. These models may require more computational time and thus more energy, although some speakers suggested that new AI tools for compression and optimization could help offset costs and energy needs. Questions such as those around latency, throughput, and multimodal models are just a few examples of the factors that contribute to significant uncertainties around future energy demands related to AI use.

SUSTAINABILITY AND SOCIETAL CONSIDERATIONS AROUND DATA CENTER EXPANSION

In addition to energy demands and related impacts on the grid, the rapid expansion of AI data centers can increase air pollution, affect water use and quality, and contribute to material use and environmental impacts from information technology equipment manufacturing and e-waste at the local, national, and global scales. Noting that data centers are already impacting the electric power grid, communities, and the environment at a speed far faster than experts can understand and quantify, Eric Masanet, University of California, Santa Barbara, highlighted the importance of building stakeholder consortia to address these issues and conduct more holistic sustainability assessments in the long term, but stressed that actions could be taken in the near term to begin to address problems. In particular, he noted that analyses of data center impacts need to incorporate factors such as water, air pollution, and e-waste along with energy and emissions impacts, and he emphasized that analyses should focus on the local scale where burdens are already being felt, since these impacts can be masked in analyses at national and global scales. At the national and global scale, many of the major tech companies, such as Google, have announced their commitment to decreasing carbon emissions from data centers.

To accomplish real improvements in environmental burden, data center operators and manufacturers of AI accelerator hardware need to be more transparent and share more information with the research community. Furthermore, Masanet highlighted the value of bridging data center energy models with life-cycle analysis approaches to provide a full life-cycle perspective. He suggested that the field could eventually move toward consequential life-cycle assessments, an approach wherein sophisticated and dynamic models of data centers' energy use and emissions consider not only direct life-cycle inputs and outputs, but also various indirect scenarios and consequences on the economy and environment. For example, this approach could be used to understand the sustainability impacts of keeping fossil fuel plants in operation in order to meet growing energy demands instead of being retired and replaced with clean technologies. Using consequential life-cycle analyses to project different scenarios can enable stakeholders to more fully understand near- and long-term impacts of various approaches and reduce adverse impacts, Masanet noted.

In a session moderated by Prashant Shenoy, University of Massachusetts Amherst, experts highlighted societal considerations around data center expansion, including opportunities for data center growth to propel grid improvements, as well as the potential for significant negative impacts on local communities. While AI applications have many potential benefits for society, including for supporting grid modernization and power management, Shenoy said that it is as yet unclear whether these benefits will outweigh the negative impacts of unchecked data center expansion. Several speakers highlighted the need for both technology advancements and policy solutions to guide responsible growth.

The scale and concentration of AI data centers influence their impacts on communities. Several speakers pointed to examples of negative impacts on air quality, water availability, land use, and electricity costs being experienced by communities in Northern Virginia, which is home to the largest concentration of data centers in the world. These negative impacts must also be weighed against the potential benefits to communities, such as tax revenue and the potential for increased grid stability if the data center is capable of flexible operation or hosting its own behind-the-meter power resources.

As AI development moves forward, speakers underscored the need to look beyond performance improvements and consider factors such as equity and sustainability implications. Shenoy suggested that developing smaller, more distributed AI data centers and inference services, similar to how content delivery and edge networks function, could help to counter trends toward hyperscaling and clustering and thereby ameliorate some of the negative impacts in communities. He added that people may also be willing to accept some sacrifices in terms of performance, such as increased latency, if it helps to avoid negative impacts to the local environment, residents, and grid infrastructure.

DATA CENTER INFRASTRUCTURE AND TECHNOLOGY ADVANCEMENT

Participants also examined how the hardware and software infrastructure that underlies AI data centers can influence future AI use, energy demands, and data centers' interactions with the grid. Ayse K. Coskun, Boston University, pointed to a need to reconsider all aspects of data center design, from hardware and software to cooling and architecture, for increased efficiency and sustainability now and in the future. Many speakers pointed to the role of flexibility in addressing these issues, including the need for flexibility to incorporate future improvements in hardware and software; flexibility to smooth out the wide swings in energy consumption that are common with some AI processes that pose a threat to grid reliability; and demand flexibility in terms of how data centers respond to external constraints or demand response programs, onsite energy availability, and carbon and cost metrics. While flexibility and demand response have great potential to address efficiency and sustainability, AI-focused data centers today often run at maximum capacity, in part due to the significant cost of AI-specific hardware.

At the same time, several technological advances are under way to improve the efficiency of AI workloads. Researchers are developing new model architectures that require fewer computational resources, such as sparse models, and are exploring smaller, task-specific models as alternatives to large, general-purpose ones. Innovations in hardware-software codesign are also yielding gains in efficiency. Additionally, advances in optical interconnects are helping reduce the energy cost of data movement within data centers, a growing contributor to overall power use. Perhaps most notably, there have been significant increases in chip efficiency in recent years, with each new generation of AI accelerators—such as graphics processing units, tensor processing units, and custom application-specific integrated circuits—delivering significant improvements in performance per watt, helping to curb the otherwise steep rise in AI-related energy consumption.

Carole-Jean Wu, Meta, underscored the role of AI as this century's most important technology, affecting every economic sector and bringing new capabilities that may help to address many important societal problems. She said that the rapidly growing energy demands associated with AI make it critical to pursue efficiency innovations across the entire AI stack, from hardware to software to infrastructure and algorithm redesigns. Scalable model architecture innovations can also create efficiencies, and a better overall understanding of AI workloads can unlock more benefits. These innovations will be especially important when easier-to-achieve AI efficiency techniques reach a point of diminishing returns, Wu noted.

Metrics can help redefine technical and policy goals as well as performance and service-level agreements. Several speakers suggested that more holistic sustainability metrics, such as metrics capturing health costs and other community impacts, are needed along with new metrics to augment or replace current power use efficiency measures and capture a broader range of sustainability goals, such as carbon emissions, water use, and flexibility.

A CALL FOR COLLABORATION AND DATA SHARING

A common thread throughout the workshop was a call for enhanced collaboration and data sharing around AI data center activities, energy use, and interactions with the grid. In terms of understanding current and future trends, Lee noted that speakers identified a need for additional data to quantify and project the benefits and harms of AI use cases and different data center designs and enable the models used for these projections to be more granular and reflective of data centers' hardware, software, and operational characteristics. While capabilities are improving, several speakers noted that the rapid growth and high level of uncertainty in this sector undermines the ability to model energy demands and make accurate projections.

Although it may be difficult to accomplish, Coskun said that more effective data sharing and collaboration among industry, academia, and government would be instrumental in improving the overall understanding of AI workloads, forecasting capabilities, and informing sustainability standards. She suggested that more collaboration and access, perhaps modeled on the Electric Power Research Institute's DCFlex initiative, can inform prototypes and early-concept demonstrations.[2]

Recognizing that the potential impacts of data centers encompass multiple domains and stakeholders—from public health practitioners to electrical engineers and grid systems operators—participants also underscored the importance of collaboration and data sharing to fully elucidate and mitigate effects of data center expansion on the grid and communities. Several participants suggested a need for companies building data centers to be more transparent about these operations to ensure accurate projections. Masanet added that experts across many areas will be needed to make use of this information. For example, engineers and technologists are needed to input the computational complexities into the models; energy and life-cycle assessment analysts are needed to extract insights from modeling; epidemiologists and community groups are needed to identify possible impacts; and social science experts are needed to incorporate behavioral and economic implications into sustainability analyses.

Facilitating flexible demand response coordination with optimized, AI-driven metrics that contribute to larger-scale grid coordination and decarbonization efforts would also require effective exchange of information and coordination between data center owners and grid operators, Wu noted. In addition, she said that there is a need for data centers and their suppliers to be more transparent in their emissions and accounting methodologies to enable accurate quantification of their environmental impacts and drive emissions reductions and energy optimizations. Finally, from a policy perspective, Shenoy noted that collaboration among community, industry, and government stakeholders is needed to design fair regulations that bring the widest possible benefits.

[2] Electric Power Research Institute, n.d., "DCFlex," https://msites.epri.com/dcflex, accessed April 21, 2025.

1

Introduction

In recent years, the global adoption of artificial intelligence (AI) has spurred significant construction and investment in new data centers and cloud computing.[1] These data centers require large-scale continuous power, posing challenges for local electric grids and broader climate goals. To explore how to map, measure, and mitigate the impacts of AI data center electricity usage, the National Academies of Sciences, Engineering, and Medicine convened the workshop Implications of Artificial Intelligence–Related Data Center Electricity Use and Emissions in Washington, DC, on November 12–13, 2024. Organized through the National Academies' Roundtable on Artificial Intelligence and Climate Change, the event gathered more than 95 in-person and more than 350 virtual participants to discuss how recent AI developments could impact energy demands, identify options to mitigate increased electricity use and emissions, and consider regional implications related to data center siting and renewable resource availability.

In opening remarks, workshop planning committee chair Benjamin C. Lee, University of Pennsylvania, described the event's overarching goal of fostering ongoing discussions, shared learning, and coordination as stakeholders from academia, industry, utilities, community advocacy groups, and government agencies work to understand and mitigate the technical, social, behavioral, and environmental impacts of AI data centers and their

[1] Cloud computing refers to the provision of computing services such as databases, storage, networking, and analytics on-demand over the Internet.

unique energy needs. He said that both technical and policy solutions will be needed to mitigate these large energy demands and their associated carbon emissions and impacts on local communities. Even as data centers pose new challenges for the electric power grid, he added that AI technologies can also potentially aid efforts to improve the grid and accelerate decarbonization goals by facilitating efficiency improvements both in data centers and across the economy more broadly.

Over the 2-day workshop, participants examined current trends and available evidence along with various sources of uncertainty and complexity relevant to emerging issues at the intersection of electric utilities and AI data centers. Three keynote speakers reviewed the state of the evidence on data center energy use, their projected power use and implications for the grid, and opportunities to achieve greater efficiency through technology advancements. In five panel discussions, experts considered trends and future use cases for AI; challenges and opportunities in data center infrastructure and hardware–software interactions; and the implications of data centers for the grid, sustainability goals, and local economies and communities. A fireside chat offered a venue for utility system operators to share their perspectives and experiences. In the event's closing session, planning committee members offered reflections on the issues discussed during the workshop and considered the roles of various stakeholders in contributing to solutions going forward. The workshop's statement of task is provided in Appendix A, the agenda is in Appendix B, and the planning committee and speaker biographies are found in Appendix C. Recordings and other materials are available at the workshop website.[2] This proceedings summarizes the workshop presentations and discussions based on transcripts and recordings from the event and does not represent the views of the National Academies.

[2] National Academies, n.d., "Implications of Artificial Intelligence-Related Data Center Electricity Use and Emissions: A Workshop," https://www.nationalacademies.org/our-work/implications-of-artificial-intelligence-related-data-center-electricity-use-and-emissions-a-workshop, accessed April 21, 2025.

2

Context on Data Center Energy Use and Impacts

Two keynote speakers reviewed emerging data to provide context on data center energy use and impacts. Arman Shehabi, Lawrence Berkeley National Laboratory (LBNL), discussed how data center energy use has evolved over the past two decades and considered how the rise of highly specialized hardware and artificial intelligence (AI) might create new opportunities for efficiency and decarbonization. Thomas Wilson, Electric Power Research Institute (EPRI), shared highlights from EPRI projections of data center power use and grid impacts and discussed how more flexible data center operations could help to accelerate AI development while minimizing costs, lowering carbon emissions, and enhancing system reliability.

THE EVOLUTION OF DATA CENTER ENERGY USE

The adoption of AI applications across multiple fields could bring significant impacts for data center energy use and the electric utilities that are responsible for supplying power across the United States. To provide context for the current trends in this space, Shehabi described a series of three reports documenting how data centers and their energy demands have evolved over the past 25 years. LBNL's bottom-up, continually evolving models provide a basis for these analyses by compiling available information about the number of servers in operation and the equipment and architectures being used for storage, networking, cooling, and other facets of data center operations to estimate energy use. The resulting reports, published in 2007,[1] 2016,[2] and 2024,[3] serve as a resource for decision makers regarding the factors that are driving the energy demands of data centers and their environmental impacts.[4]

Congress first requested that LBNL analyze data center electricity use and opportunities to mitigate this trajectory in energy demand in the early 2000s, driven by a concern that, if current trends at the time were to continue, data centers could account for one-third of all U.S. energy use by 2030.[5] As the 2007 report documented, data centers' electricity use had doubled from 2000–2005.[6] Shehabi explained that this large energy demand was due to an increased buildout of data centers but also in part to operational inefficiencies; during the initial years of the dot-com expansion, data centers were built with off-the-shelf equipment, cooling methods were not optimized for efficiency, and idle servers drew large amounts of power. By the 2010s, as documented in the 2016 report, data centers were much larger, but their energy demands remained relatively flat thanks to the adoption of more energy-efficient custom equipment, advancements in cooling technologies, and a shift toward cloud services.[7]

Following these periods of rising and then plateauing energy demand, recent years have seen another turning point characterized by a sharp rise in data center energy demands (Figure 2-1). This shift can be largely attributed to the growth of AI, which has increased the need for graphics processing unit (GPU) accelerators, increased power draws from servers, and spurred a shift from smaller data centers to clustered and hyperscale ones. These factors combined to essentially triple energy

---

[1] R. Brown, E. Masanet, B. Norman, et al., 2008, *Report to Congress on Server and Data Center Energy Efficiency: Public Law 109-431*, Lawrence Berkeley National Laboratory, https://escholarship.org/uc/item/74g2r0vg.

[2] A. Shehabi, S. Smith, D. Sartor, et al., 2016, *United States Data Center Energy Usage Report*, LBNL-1005775, Lawrence Berkeley National Laboratory, https://www.iea-4e.org/wp-content/uploads/publications/2016/06/05j_-_LBNL_-_US_Data_Centres_Energy_USe.pdf.

[3] A. Shehabi, S.J. Smith, A. Hubbard, et al., 2024, *2024 United States Data Center Energy Usage Report*, LBNL-2001637, Lawrence Berkeley National Laboratory, https://eta-publications.lbl.gov/sites/default/files/2024-12/lbnl-2024-united-states-data-center-energy-usage-report.pdf.

[4] A. Shehabi, S.J. Smith, E. Masanet, and J. Koomey, 2018, "Data Center Growth in the United States: Decoupling the Demand for Services from Electricity Use," *Environmental Research Letters* 13(12):124030, https://doi.org/10.1088/1748-9326/aaec9c.

[5] E. Masanet, A. Shehabi, N. Lei, S. Smith, and J. Koomey, 2020, "Recalibrating Global Data Center Energy-Use Estimates," *Science* 367(6481):984–986, https://doi.org/10.1126/science.aba3758.

[6] J.G. Koomey, 2008, "Worldwide Electricity Used in Data Centers," *Environmental Research Letters* 3(3):034008, https://doi.org/10.1088/1748-9326/3/3/034008.

[7] A. Shehabi, S. Smith, D. Sartor, et al., 2016, *United States Data Center Energy Usage Report*, LBNL-1005775, Lawrence Berkeley National Laboratory, https://www.iea-4e.org/wp-content/uploads/publications/2016/06/05j_-_LBNL_-_US_Data_Centres_Energy_USe.pdf.

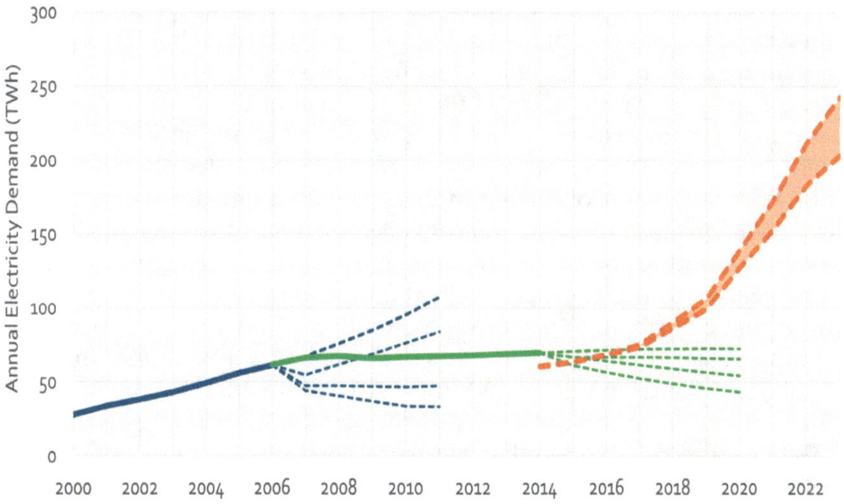

FIGURE 2-1 Estimated annual electricity demand from data centers in the United States, 2000–2023. Blue and green lines represent estimated (solid lines) and projected (dashed lines) electricity use in reports from Lawrence Berkeley National Laboratory published in 2007 (blue) and 2016 (green). Dashed orange lines and shading represent preliminary estimates in a 2024 report.
SOURCE: Arman Shehabi, Lawrence Berkeley National Laboratory, presentation to the workshop, November 12, 2024.

demand between 2017 and 2023—and may triple it again in the next few years,[8] Shehabi said.

Developments in data center operations occur alongside and interact with broader societal trends in the economy and the ways in which people use technology. Shehabi pointed out that the plateau in data center energy use that was documented in the 2016 report began around the time of the 2008 recession, while the rapid growth that has occurred since 2017 was driven in part by the growth of social media, which further accelerated during the COVID-19 pandemic. While early efficiency innovations offset data centers' energy impact, their rapid growth soon outpaced both efficiency gains and clean energy expansion, leading to rising energy demand and emissions.

---

[8] R. Miller, 2024, "DOE Study: AI Boom Breeds Localized Energy Constraints, But Grid Can Meet Long-Term Demand," Data Center Frontier, https://www.datacenterfrontier.com/energy/article/55019791/doe-study-ai-boom-breeds-localized-energy-constraints-but-grid-can-meet-long-term-demand.

Models can be useful in understanding drivers of past trends and projecting future ones, but Shehabi cautioned that models are not perfect, the future remains uncertain, and many factors could affect what happens next. Data center growth could flatten again after this latest acceleration, or it may continue to grow as AI improves and constraints, such as chip and energy availability, are removed. Shehabi also noted that the growth of AI data centers is occurring in parallel with a broader economy-wide expansion in electricity demand propelled by trends toward electrification in transportation and onshoring of manufacturing, and suggested that AI data centers could serve as a testbed and resource to help drive innovations that contribute to responsible growth in energy use and decarbonization goals. "I think data centers are, in many ways, a great first type of industry for us to figure out how we can deal with this type of growth that we are going to have to deal with many times over," Shehabi said. "Data centers relative to other industrial loads are quite flexible in their location and in how they can adjust their power. They're innovative industrial players, and they have interests in decarbonization." In light of both the potential opportunities and the uncertainties that lie ahead, Shehabi underscored the importance of continuing to study data centers' energy use and their impact on the grid.

An open question-and-answer session followed Shehabi's presentation. Trisha Ray, Atlantic Council, asked if LBNL's modeling approaches accounted for climate events such as droughts and flooding. Shehabi replied that modelers do account for how factors such as droughts and general warming might affect cooling systems; however, he noted that it is challenging to project more than a few years into the future.

Andrew Chien, University of Chicago, commented that there remain many barriers to creating accurate modeling estimates and forecasts and informing greater coordination around investment in power, transmission, and data center infrastructure. Shehabi agreed and noted that one of the biggest challenges has been the lack of transparency in data center energy use and growth compared to other industries. If that information could be securely shared, the models' accuracy would improve. Sarah Medepalli, Noblis, asked if any intergovernmental or research-based collaborative efforts were tasked with addressing the increased energy needs associated with AI. Shehabi replied that there are at least a few such efforts that are in their early stages, citing the Congressional AI Task Force and the Department of Energy's (DOE's) AI Task Force as two examples.

Andrew Grimshaw, Lancium and University of Virginia, noted that when electricity costs and the cost of carbon emissions are low, companies will use as much energy as they need to accomplish their performance goals. While efficiency is seen as a good thing, he asked whether increasing energy use should always be perceived as a negative outcome.

Shehabi noted that electrification and growing the grid to aid decarbonization efforts is a widely embraced goal but emphasized the need to make that growth clean and sustainable and avoid reverting to fossil fuels. He suggested that data centers can lead the way to enabling broader clean energy buildouts that will ultimately support the power needs of other industries. Kurt Straif, Boston College, asked how to balance increased electricity use with the urgent need to reduce carbon emissions, and Shehabi replied that data center growth offers an opportunity to accelerate decarbonization, since data centers are an industry that is already electrified and poised to drive strategic grid growth, potentially creating a path to more clean energy.

Tracy Wilson, OTH Analysis LLC, asked how chip design or quantum computing advances could influence future growth, and Shehabi agreed that such innovations could be game changers. However, while chips are increasingly computationally efficient, he emphasized that increased efficiency does not necessarily equate to reduced energy needs given the seemingly unlimited demand for computation. "Being able to compute more with the same amount of power just allows us to compute more," he stated.

Prakhar Mehrotra, Blackstone, asked about the relative influence of inference versus training[9] in driving the energy use trends Shehabi described in the late 2000s and early 2010s and looking toward the future. Shehabi reiterated that the flat demand seen during that period was driven by the economic recession combined with new efficiencies such as those enabled by the shift to cloud computing. Looking to the future, he said that a shift of a similar magnitude in the energy use trajectory would require a similarly groundbreaking innovation that fundamentally changes how data centers operate.

PROJECTED DATA CENTER POWER USE AND IMPLICATIONS FOR THE GRID

Wilson highlighted findings from several EPRI reports and initiatives focused on the intersection of U.S. energy systems and data centers over the coming years. The 2024 report *Powering Intelligence: Analyzing Artificial Intelligence and Data Center Energy Consumption*[10] examines how

[9] Inference is the use of an AI model to generate outputs such as conclusions or predictions; training is the process of teaching an AI model to make inferences by recognizing patterns in data.

[10] Electric Power Research Institute (EPRI), 2024, "Powering Intelligence: Analyzing Artificial Intelligence and Data Center Energy Consumption," https://www.epri.com/research/products/3002028905.

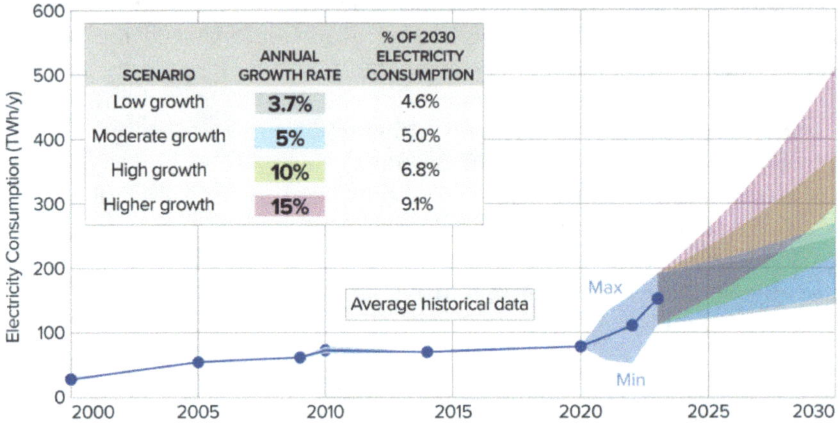

FIGURE 2-2 Projected growth in U.S. data center demands through 2030 under four scenarios.
SOURCE: Tom Wilson, EPRI, presentation to the workshop, November 12, 2024.

data centers drive electricity demand, opportunities for efficiency gains or growth limits, and projections for future demand. The report outlines four scenarios for data center power demands through 2030 (Figure 2-2), while acknowledging the wide range of uncertainties involved in making these projections. To complement and expand upon national-level estimates, Wilson also stressed the importance of the rapid shift to larger data centers and potentially significant implications for local and regional grids. Companies consider a variety of factors when determining where to site data centers, including power availability, the presence of a local technology market, fiber connectivity, local taxes and energy costs, land availability, and access to low-carbon energy options. While data centers were historically highly concentrated in a few locations, Wilson noted that they have become more geographically distributed in recent years—with Virginia home to by far the largest concentration, followed by Beijing and emerging locations such as Oregon and Phoenix (Figure 2-3).[11]

In another report, a survey of representatives from 25 electric utility operators offers insights on the volume and nature of data center interconnection requests utilities were seeing in the summer of 2024. Respondents reported that companies are requesting larger interconnects,

[11] J. Albers, V. Dahiya, A. Fraym, and J. Howe, 2024, *2024 Global Data Center Market Comparison*, Cushman & Wakefield, https://www.cushmanwakefield.com/en/insights/global-data-center-market-comparison.

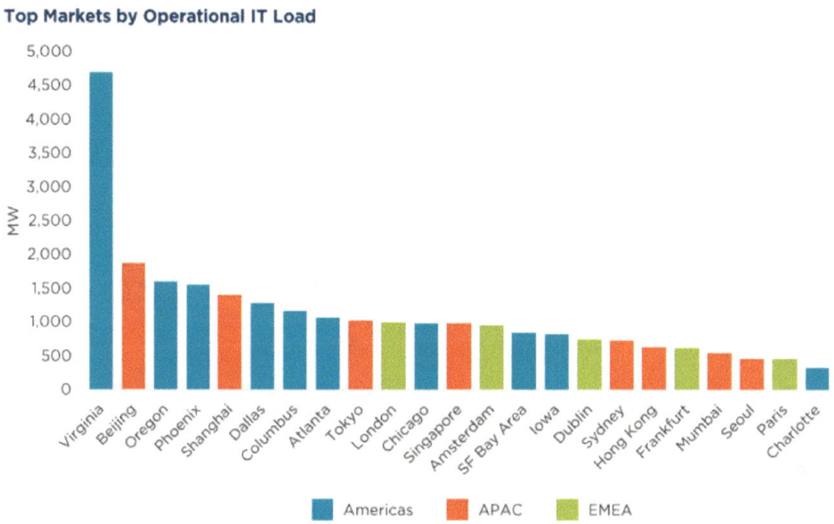

FIGURE 2-3 Operational information technology load by market.
NOTE: APAC, Asia-Pacific; EMEA, Europe, the Middle East, and Africa.
SOURCES: Tom Wilson, EPRI, presentation to the workshop, November 12, 2024, from Cushman & Wakefield, "2024 Global Data Center Market Comparison," https://www.cushmanwakefield.com/en/insights/global-data-center-market-comparison.

with 60 percent seeing requests for single sites of 500 MW or larger and 48 percent seeing requests for 1000 MW or larger.[12] Data centers are also expected to account for an increasingly large fraction of system peak demand. Even acknowledging that there are many duplicated requests for interconnection, respondents reported that the magnitude of requests is massive, exceeding current system peak demands for 5 of the 22 respondents and exceeding by 2.5-fold the current system peak demand of 1 respondent.

Another report, *Powering Data Centers: U.S. Energy System and Emissions Impacts of Growing Loads*, examines the implications of data center load growth for power generation and emissions, considering both a current policy scenario and a future where the United States is committed to achieving net-zero emissions by 2050. In addition to load growth from data centers, the study considered increased loads from electrification

---

[12] EPRI, 2024, "Utility Experiences and Trends Regarding Data Centers: 2024 Survey," https://www.epri.com/research/products/000000003002030643.

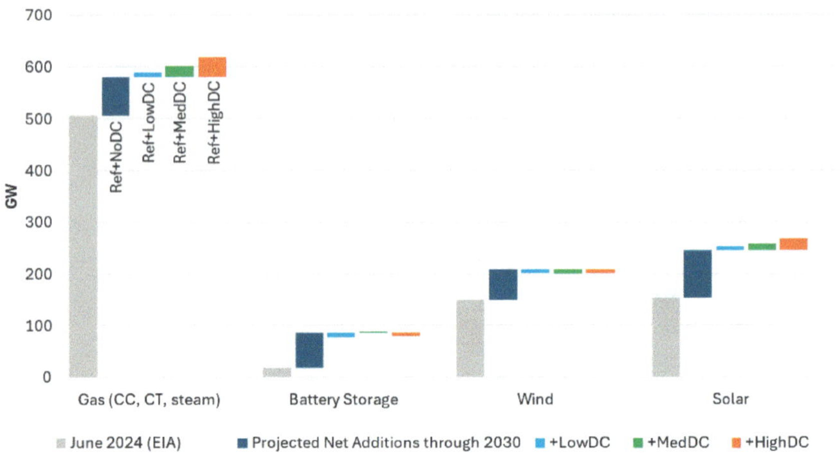

FIGURE 2-4 Projected capacity additions through 2030 for gas, battery storage, wind, and solar under different data center growth scenarios. Grey bars indicate current capacity (through June 2024); colored bars indicate projected additional capacity assuming no, low, medium, and high data center load growth scenarios. SOURCE: Tom Wilson, EPRI, presentation to the workshop, November 12, 2024.

and industrial on-shoring.[13] The report's projections of net additions to energy generation and storage capacity through 2030 under different load growth scenarios suggest that additional natural gas and solar generation capacity will provide most of the new capacity, with wind and battery storage accounting for a lower share (Figure 2-4), assuming data centers focused on least-cost electricity supply. Wilson noted that if data center owners achieved voluntary goals, such as hourly matching of their load with carbon-free energy, emissions impacts would be reduced as storage technologies and carbon-free resources, such as nuclear, play larger roles.

Wilson also pointed out that if data centers can operate flexibly (either through computational flexibility or by utilizing onsite storage or generation resources in times of grid stress), grid buildout could be reduced, and it is possible to meet more of these demands with renewable energy and avoid additional fossil fuel use. However, there are many questions to resolve in order to realize that vision of flexible data centers. To advance work in this area, EPRI recently launched the Data Center Flexible Load Initiative (DCFlex) in collaboration with a large group of technology

[13] EPRI, 2024, "Powering Data Centers: U.S. Energy System and Emissions Impacts of Growing Loads," white paper, https://www.epri.com/research/products/000000003002031198.

industry stakeholders, data center developers, equipment suppliers, and electric power companies, which include utilities, independent power producers, independent system operators, and regional transmission organizations. The initiative aims to create reference architectures for flexible data centers that can become grid enhancers, identify transformative utility programs and new market structures that incentivize data center flexibility, and design a flexibility framework with a standardized taxonomy for grid-data center communications and operations to avoid reliability challenges and system failures.[14]

Following Wilson's remarks, participants delved deeper into issues around modeling, flexibility, and costs. Chien asked about the emissions connected with each of the capacity growth scenarios EPRI modeled, and Wilson stated that the numbers are in the report.[15] They generally suggest that emissions will rise as data center demand increases through about 2030, but this bump will be followed by a contraction by around 2035 as technological advancements come online to create a cleaner grid. How this plays out depends on the policies in place to incentivize renewables or flexibility, limit increased coal or gas generation, and mitigate emissions impacts to communities hosting data centers, he added. Shehabi asked if data centers are actually using the increased capacity utilities are bringing online now, or whether it is being purchased with the idea that it would be used in the future. Wilson replied that the answer is unclear, but given that there are essentially waiting lists for GPU time, data centers probably are using it as soon as they can get it. However, he noted that that could change as capacity ramps up, and ramp-up of power demands may depend on data centers' different ownership models.

George Kamiya, an independent expert, asked what utility administrators can do to leverage data center load as a flexible resource. Wilson replied that computational flexibility can facilitate geographic or temporal redispatching of workloads. While onsite backup generation can create additional flexibility when grid reliability is a concern, he noted that there are air quality impacts and operational limitations if diesel-powered generators are used for this. He also noted that arbitrage over limited variation in electricity prices is unlikely to incentivize change, but shorter connection or in-service times create strong incentives for data centers to build in flexibility. Giri Iyer, Sentient Energy, asked what innovations can improve solar and wind dispatchability and affordability, and Wilson replied that pairing batteries with solar can shift generation across hours in the day, but that did not work as well for wind, generally speaking. Will

[14] EPRI, n.d., "DCFlex," https://msites.epri.com/dcflex, accessed April 21, 2025.

[15] EPRI, 2024, "Powering Data Centers: U.S. Energy System and Emissions Impacts of Growing Loads," white paper, https://www.epri.com/research/products/000000003002031198.

Bryant, ClearPath, asked if EPRI had any reliability or pricing concerns with the wind and solar data used in their reports. Wilson reiterated that the data and models are incomplete—for example, they do not include uncertain weather, resource adequacy, or reliability modeling—and said that more discussion and analysis is needed.

Lee pointed out that a critical question is, Who should bear the costs and hosting responsibilities of flexibility initiatives: data centers or utilities? Wilson replied that discussions of that question are just starting, both in the United States and globally, and companies are only beginning to consider the potential business cases and risks. Reid Lifset, Yale University, asked what the impacts on consumer electricity prices might be, and Wilson replied that retail rates were not a large focus of EPRI's modeling in this paper. The analysis showed a large increase in electricity load with costs per kilowatt hour staying roughly the same. He added that who pays for this is an important issue with implications for fairness, although this was not an area that was addressed by the EPRI analysis.

3

Artificial Intelligence Technologies: Trends and Future Use Cases

The ways in which artificial intelligence (AI) technologies are used will influence the future impact of AI data centers on electricity use and computing resource demands. Benjamin Lee, University of Pennsylvania, moderated a session examining the trajectory of AI, taking a holistic view of considerations related to data processing, training, and inference.

The panel's two speakers, Eric Xing of Carnegie Mellon University and Prakhar Mehrotra of Blackstone, briefly described their respective backgrounds before launching into a discussion moderated by Lee. Mehrotra's current work focuses on bringing AI capabilities to the more than 200 companies in Blackstone's portfolio; previously, he worked in applied AI at Walmart, Uber, and Twitter. Xing's work spans fundamental AI research and AI applications. He spoke about his work to improve embodied and counterfactual reasoning of multi-agent models toward a goal of creating AI systems that are capable of complex inferences and reasoning beyond language, which will be needed in order to advance the application of AI to fields such as biology, physics, and social behaviors, where features such as biological structures, the physics of liquids, or the nuances of gaming behavior are not captured in words. He also highlighted the importance of working to reduce the energy costs of running AI data centers but noted that energy use is often secondary to the drive to rapidly produce and improve AI models.

PANEL DISCUSSION

The panelists discussed the capabilities, opportunities, and costs of large language models (LLMs);[1] factors that could affect future AI use cases such as latency, hallucinations, and energy needs; and considerations around open-source models and data sharing. As context for the discussion, Mehrotra noted that LLMs have evolved several times, from feature engineering to neural networks to transformer architecture, to arrive at their current status as a fundamental building block for many AI tools. Because today's LLMs are pre-trained and broadly accessible, they create a level playing field for using AI without requiring the technical expertise needed to understand how they work or build a model from scratch. Xing added that the architecture and design of LLMs have been largely stable for the past several years. Advancements have made the models much larger and more powerful, but there are still limitations around tokenization, embedding, attention, training loss, and algorithm design. In addition, because the inferencing capabilities are dependent on memorization and autoregression, he noted that the cost-to-return ratio will diminish as sources of textual data are exhausted.

MODEL SIZES AND CUSTOMIZATION

Looking forward, Mehrotra suggested that the next generation of AI technologies is likely to bring LLMs that are smaller, more domain-specific, and more accurate, potentially fueling paradigm shifts across many fields. Lee wondered if specialized, domain-specific LLMs might be more energy efficient than large, general-purpose models, and Mehrotra replied that the answer is unknown. Businesses will need domain-specific LLMs, but there is not yet a cost-effective pathway to create and continually train them. General-purpose LLMs are still in their early stages and will need at least a few more years to provide adequate accuracy, and while a consumer using an LLM for personal or entertainment purposes can accept wrong answers, a business cannot. "The only metric that matters in the enterprise setting is how good your results are," Mehrotra stated.

Lee asked what additional costs might be associated with domain-specific training for LLMs. Xing replied that domain-specific models have very different economics than large-scale LLMs with their trillions of parameters, which can be challenging to fine-tune. Smaller models, with only billions of parameters, are easier to fine-tune and may not need to rely on existing LLMs. For example, specialized models can regain the performance of LLMs with an architecture that is continuously incrementable

[1] LLMs are AI programs that can understand and generate text. ChatGPT is one example.

and growable, enabling additional components to be harmonized for more capabilities.

Ayse Coskun, Boston University, prompted panelists to delve deeper into the pros and cons of large, general models versus customizing domain-specific, smaller models that can be installed locally. Mehrotra said that both types of models have value and speculated that eventually a hybrid system will develop in which consumers use general LLMs to handle requests and work in multiple modalities, while business, research, and other domain-specific users will want smaller, custom models that can be fine-tuned and learn continually. In fact, edge computing could operate on much smaller models that fit on a smartphone, creating a latency advantage. In this scenario, latency and privacy could become the deciding factors in determining which model sizes are optimal.

Xing agreed that there is not one "best" size for an AI model and added that sometimes a system's optimal size is defined by the hardware environment. Seventy billion parameters is often used because it fits on one graphics processing unit (GPU), but having multiple GPUs solves that problem. He also highlighted a variety of other factors that currently pose a barrier to progress in developing custom or domain-specific models, including a limited workforce with the skills needed to fine-tune models; a lack of industrial standards for data format, interfacing, or transfer; and a lack of coordination across silos, which makes it challenging to create standards, general practices, and training curricula. In response to a question from Ataliba Miguel, TotalEnergies, Lee noted that fine-tuning today is too idiosyncratic to lend itself to a universal approach, and more workforce training is needed. Mehrotra agreed and also pushed for fine-tuning standards.

Jonathan Herz, Environmental and Energy Study Institute, asked if the situation faced with AI systems today could be similar to the way computer operating systems have historically been built on layers of energy-hungry building blocks, resulting in decreasing efficiency over time. Mehrotra replied that LLMs are building blocks of multi-agent systems that can accomplish multiple tasks that today are completed by software. Agent-driven decisions will increase energy costs because of the many steps involved and the potentially large number of users, but the tasks themselves will become easier and more efficient. Xing added that today's AI models are very different from classic software engineering, which has clear definitions and cost-effectiveness measures that eventually reach a point of diminishing returns. Such limitations are not yet apparent for AI, which he speculated will not see a big emphasis on cost efficiency until it is commercially viable and scientifically valuable. He expressed his belief that experimentation with AI will lead to surprising functions and discoveries beyond what we can envision today. Lee agreed that one reason AI systems are not experiencing "software bloat"[2] is because their boundaries and capabilities are still expanding. However, he reiterated that there are many uncertainties around the costs of training LLMs in order to discover their capabilities and create smaller, specialized models for effective domain-specific inferencing.

Modalities Beyond Language

Xing added that another opportunity is to use LLMs as foundations for image, audio, and other modalities by optimizing interfacing tokenization processes, or the ability to encode text into smaller units. By focusing on interface optimization as opposed to building new models from scratch for each modality, multimodal LLMs can be more cost effective. Lee asked how this approach would impact the training costs, computational load, and electricity use for AI systems. Xing replied that computational load inefficiencies could be improved by learning from cognitive science findings and applying attention and tokenization differently depending on what information is being received. The transformers and attention arrays of current LLMs cannot do this but instead homogeneously apply attention to all signals. Heterogeneous attention mechanisms, along with data quantization and compression schemes, could be exploited to more efficiently understand the signal, Xing suggested. He also added that training loss is another area that can be improved by looking at human learning patterns. In the next few years, he speculated that new LLM architectures and learning mechanisms will reduce costs without compromising performance, enabling the development of non-language models and multimodal LLMs. Human brain–inspired architectures are still nascent but have enormous potential to be more energy-efficient and adaptive—current LLMs must activate every parameter for every task, whereas brain-inspired models could use only necessary parameters, making storage and retrieval of knowledge more efficient.

Mehrotra cautioned that adding video as a modality is incredibly complicated because it is three-dimensional, has multiple frames, and requires temporal attention. There might not be an existing transformer architecture to support those capabilities. However, a major strength of today's LLMs is their high degree of flexibility, with low generalization error rates for low-complexity tasks. Human cognition is far more complicated, but machines have internal patterns that can be automated to

---

[2] *Software bloat* is a process where new versions of a computer program become successively slower, use more memory or processing power, or have more hardware requirements than previous versions as new features are added.

mitigate the new demands on the grid as every sector looks to train and fine-tune LLMs. To bend or flatten this demand, he suggested that businesses will either revert to older machine learning paradigms that have improved accuracy, which requires time and resources, or seek architecture and chip advances that create efficiencies.

Artificial Intelligence for Scientific Discovery

Valerie Taylor, Argonne National Laboratory, asked about the potential to use LLMs to train AI-powered scientific assistants in different disciplines. Xing replied that foundational LLMs are inadequate for science because they only process language—and biological data, such as gene expression or protein structures, are not adequately captured in human language. New models with dedicated architectures, bandwidths, and inferences are needed to understand scientific data. Nevertheless, Xing suggested that general LLMs can be used for some areas of scientific inquiry as researchers learn how to best phrase a query, and those LLMs could then engage with or evolve into more useful multimodal models. In the meantime, many AI tools for scientific research have been created, and although they are still experimental, they have been useful and are attracting more attention. "I see that as a huge inspiration and acknowledgement and confirmation of the value of AI in science, but it's just a starting point," Xing stated. "The next few years will see a big uptick."

Mehrotra added that AI is already useful in the literature review phase of research, boosting productivity and suggesting new ideas as scientists formulate research questions and design experiments. For hypothesis-building, AI tools can also help narrow the search space and validate hypotheses. In the experimental and validation phases, however, fine-tuning and customized models will be needed, and Mehrotra said that the technology in this space is not yet mature.

Factors Affecting Inference and Artificial Intelligence Adoption

Panelists explored how demands related to AI training differ from those stemming from inference, along with factors that may affect inference demand, scale, and efficiency in the future. Lee stated that LLMs will continue to be trained, specialized, and fine-tuned, but it is unclear how AI data centers' costs and energy usage will change once they move from the high fixed costs incurred during training to the variable costs and energy demands of inference as LLMs become more widely used. Mehrotra replied that inference is in its earliest phases, and there are currently only a few examples of inference workloads, such as ChatGPT, Llama, and Gemini. Their key energy metric is not training but concurrent users. If that number grows to the millions or tens of millions, much more equipment and replication will be needed in order to keep latency[3] low. Latency is also impacted by how many steps an AI model needs to answer a question. Mehrotra noted that latencies are often in the milliseconds, and those longer than 1–2 seconds were once considered unacceptable, but experience has shown that in the case of AI, users are more tolerant of latency—being willing to wait 25–30 seconds for a result—and allowing for more latency could enable alternative inferencing designs. In inferencing, there is not one single metric to measure performance, and so multiple factors, such as chip type or GPU supply, could be altered to impact latency. However, Mehrotra said that uncertainties in terms of the number of concurrent users, the steps needed to answer a question, and the acceptable latency range complicates the task of creating inference optimizations and efficiencies.

Prompted by a question from Trisha Ray, Atlantic Council, regarding users' willingness to accept latency, Xing said that it is too early to know what latency levels will be acceptable to users and this is likely to change as AI—and the public's expectations—rapidly evolve. Mehrotra added that when AI is used to answer questions or perform calculations that would be infeasible for humans to solve without AI tools, people are likely to be willing to accept higher latency. Xing speculated that the acceptable latency for chatbot applications may be different from that of physical-world applications of AI, such as home robots or autonomous cars. He said that such applications will be federated but distributed, with different latency and self-learning demands that blur the boundaries between training and inference.

Lee agreed that both latency and throughput[4] connect to fundamental issues of computing performance and capabilities and that these are currently in flux, making it challenging to predict future AI use and impacts. In addition, it is unclear what total bandwidth AI systems might require, since this will be heavily influenced by how models are used. If humans are inputting prompts, the total bandwidth will be constrained by the speed at which humans can type, for example, whereas the bandwidth would be on a different order of magnitude if AI agents are inputting prompts.

Caitlin Grady, George Washington University, asked how the phenomenon of AI hallucinations might impact the acceptance and uptake of AI and the associated energy demands. Mehrotra replied that hallucinations increase energy costs because more prompts are needed to find the right answer. These extra steps do not seem to put people off, however, because

[3] *Latency* is the amount of time it takes for a system to provide a response to a user.

[4] *Throughput* is the number of queries that a system can respond to per second.

AI has still proven itself useful and hallucinations are relatively easy to correct. He added that it would be useful to conduct research into how humans perceive AI, when it is correct and when it is hallucinating. Xing added that AI hallucinations are often obvious to humans, and they are an important part of the AI learning process but also indicate that AI output should not be taken as truth. He said that an alternative technique, uncertainty quantification, could improve researchers' understanding of errors and help navigate outcome uncertainties.

Costs, Energy Use, and Future Trends

Xing noted that inference costs have gone down dramatically, much more so than training costs, because inferencing is more flexible and amorphous. Lee added that it is as yet unclear how the costs of developing and running AI systems might be passed on to consumers. Xing said that currently, inference is essentially used mostly for entertainment because its market is not fully established; however, he speculated that it will ultimately become more valuable as companies use it to augment and optimize their business. This type of use will lead to savings that companies would be willing to pay for and could offset the large costs of creating and running AI models. If AI is used to produce videos, for example, that saves studios money, similar to how virtual meetings require bandwidth but reduce air travel.

Julie Bolthouse, Piedmont Environmental Council, asked if it was possible to resolve the disconnect between the available power supply and AI data centers' demand. Xing expressed his belief that this issue will resolve itself as companies move away from the free, experimental phase and start monetizing AI products, changing their dynamic with energy providers. AI is excellent at complex math problems but still fails common sense tests, proving that LLMs need more training and perhaps more modalities, but Xing expressed confidence that they will soon achieve the capabilities and level of accuracy that will spur broader adoption. Mehrotra agreed that AI is in its early stages and much of the current energy demand is from training models, not inferencing, and significantly more training will be necessary to overcome challenges such as scaling and multimodal inputs and outputs. He opined that it remains to be seen whether multimodal models may one day achieve artificial general intelligence (AGI), a type of AI that matches or surpasses human cognition, but claims about the plausibility of AGI remain disputed and controversial.

Lee stated that this path is common for technological innovations, where the technology arrives before the "killer apps" are identified. The result is that AI and its energy costs are in a period of massive investment amid much uncertainty. In 5–10 years, Mehrotra speculated that

AI will be fully integrated into everyone's personal and professional life as a productivity instrument, but still training to achieve AGI. Xing agreed, adding that AI tools can drive paradigm shifts in business, science, research, and daily life, increasing productivity while freeing up more time for leisure activities.

Considerations for Open-Source Models and Data Sharing

Jason Hick, Los Alamos National Laboratory, asked panelists whether open-source AI models and more data sharing could encourage collaborations that include more stakeholders. Xing agreed, emphasizing that researchers need access to open source LLMs and their training mechanisms to test and replicate them. However, today's LLMs are owned by businesses, giving the academic community very little access to them except as pre-trained models. The result of this is that many academics lack a basic understanding of LLMs, which impedes their ability to improve their energy efficiency, architecture, or training paradigms. "I'm not sure whether the industry really has a full incentive to prioritize that [openness], because there is a pressure to make revenues and to advance new versions, but the academics who have the incentives of doing that, unfortunately, are not given resources and opportunity and accessibility," said Xing.

As the field moves toward fine-tuning high-quality data for user-specific applications, Xing suggested that creating open-source LLMs would provide researchers with the resources and opportunities to make improvements. AI is expensive and fast-moving, and he posited that the academic community has a responsibility to advocate against closed LLMs and promote access to fully open models to create visibility and cohesion on shared goals. To that end, his team launched a fully open-source LLM for research purposes,[5] a step he characterized as "just a start" of what he believes to be a necessary investment of effort outside of industry and for-profit LLMs to systematically share LLMs and foundation model training. Mehrotra added that AI began as an open-source product. While most models are currently closed, he speculated that at some point that will shift and the models will become open source again.

[5] See LLM360, n.d., "LLM360 Enables Community-Owned AI Through Open-Source Large Model Research and Development," https://www.llm360.ai, accessed December 15, 2024.

4

Impact of Data Centers on the Grid

As grid operators work to anticipate and meet growing demands from artificial intelligence (AI) data centers, they face a variety of challenges in forecasting needs, expanding capacity, and maintaining reliability. Participants examined these issues in a panel discussion of the increasing impact of large data centers on the grid and in a fireside chat highlighting the on-the-ground experiences of utilities.

PANELIST REMARKS

Thomas Wilson, Electric Power Research Institute (EPRI), moderated a panel on the impact of data centers on the grid and introduced the speakers: Costa Samaras, Carnegie Mellon University; Line Roald, University of Wisconsin–Madison; T. Bruce Tsuchida, Brattle Group; and Ravi Jain, Tapestry.

Advancing Climate and Energy Goals with Ethical Artificial Intelligence

Despite the many unknowns surrounding the impacts of AI data centers on the electric power grid, Samaras posited that it is still possible to achieve net-zero emissions as well as energy affordability, reliability, and resilience. "Even if we don't know everything, we can still take actions that are consistent with the outcomes that we want," he said. Analyses suggest that AI workloads in practice are overestimated by looking at the capacity of existing data centers, which is encouraging because it means there is perhaps more time to address energy issues than would be assumed based on the maximum thermal design power for the number of chips that are in use.[1] However, this only buys a little bit of time, and there remain many important issues to address.

One challenge is that AI workloads are far more variable and have much wider swings in energy use than traditional computing, which makes them computationally efficient but disruptive to the electric grid. There are various possible solutions that could help to smooth these volatile loads—by adding harmonics, addressing quality issues, building virtual power plants (VPPs),[2,3] or designing new algorithms. However, to spur progress in this space, Samaras said that it will be important to have more transparency into data centers' energy use and assess how they affect resilience and sustainability.

Samaras outlined a set of principles for ethical AI that attend to climate and energy goals, proposing that AI data centers should be net-zero, avoid adding local pollution, and add more clean power to the grid than they use; share open data and rising efficiency targets; invest in new infrastructure that increases reliability, flexibility, and resilience; avoid impacts on consumer rates; and develop community benefits agreements.[4] "I'm confident that if we center principles around people, equity, and emissions, we will be in a better place 10 years later after the broader adoption of artificial intelligence," Samaras concluded.

The Role of Data Centers in Creating a Greener Grid

Roald discussed opportunities for AI data centers to help the grid operate more economically, efficiently, sustainably, and reliably through demand response and market participation. Roald presented an analysis of how data centers can adapt their energy needs to consume power when electricity is generated with low-carbon sources. To provide the necessary feedback, this strategy would require a new carbon-intensity signal indicating when the grid is "green." There are different approaches to measure the "greenness" of electricity, including average carbon emissions,

[1] A.C. Newkirk, J. Fernandez, J. Koomey, et al., 2025, "Empirically-Calibrated H100 Node Power Models for Reducing Uncertainty in AI Training Energy Estimation," Carnegie Mellon University, https://doi.org/10.48550/arXiv.2506.14551.

[2] Virtual power plants are systems that aggregate and coordinate energy production and distribution from large collections of small energy producers.

[3] A.C. Newkirk, J. Fernandez, J. Koomey, et al., 2025, "Empirically-Calibrated H100 Node Power Models for Reducing Uncertainty in AI Training Energy Estimation," Carnegie Mellon University, https://doi.org/10.48550/arXiv.2506.14551.

[4] The White House, n.d., "Blueprint for an AI Bill of Rights," https://bidenwhitehouse.archives.gov/ostp/ai-bill-of-rights, accessed February 15, 2025.

computed by dividing total emissions by total consumption at different timescales, or marginal carbon emissions, computed by dividing changes in emissions by changes in consumption. Both methods have benefits and drawbacks and, importantly, adapting power consumption according to either of these metrics could increase stress on the grid or emissions, underscoring the need for more research in this area.[5]

Perhaps a better opportunity for data centers to support a more sustainable and reliable grid, Roald suggested, is by implementing incentivized, improved computing flexibilities that enable them to participate in the electricity market. In this scenario, data centers would make bids based on real-time usage, allowing them access to cheaper (and typically greener) electricity. This flexibility saves money for the data centers, improves grid stability, and enables data centers to actively shape carbon and price signals themselves, Roald said.

Forecasting and Meeting Electric Demand

Tsuchida discussed opportunities and challenges in forecasting future demand for electric power and preparing the grid to meet future needs. Data centers are just one of many drivers of increasing electricity demand; other major drivers include onshoring and industrial electrification, cryptocurrency mining, and increasing electrification of buildings and vehicles. While there are different projections of future load, all predict significant growth.[6]

A key challenge is to determine how accurate these forecasts are and then price energy and build services accordingly. Overestimating future loads can lead to higher utility rates, while underestimating them has multiple negative consequences, including reduced reliability. Demand response is one strategy to keep costs lower, but it is challenging for utilities to price and serve new large loads when there is so much uncertainty. Tsuchida underscored the importance of explicitly considering options for expansion in all generation and transmission plans, including through optimizing the usage of existing infrastructure, such as through the adoption of grid-enhancing technologies,[7] and incorporating the full effects of demand-side resources and non-wire alternatives.

---

[5] J. Gorka, N. Rhodes, and L. Roald, 2025, "ElectricityEmissions.jl: A Framework for the Comparison of Carbon Intensity Signals," arXiv:2411.06560, https://doi.org/10.48550/arXiv.2411.06560.

[6] T.B. Tsuchida, L. Lam, P. Fox-Penner, et al., 2024, *Electricity Demand Growth and Forecasting in a Time of Change*, The Brattle Group, https://www.brattle.com/wp-content/uploads/2024/05/Electricity-Demand-Growth-and-Forecasting-in-a-Time-of-Change-1.pdf.

[7] Grid-enhancing technologies include various hardware and software tools that help to alleviate congestion and control the flow of power through the electric grid.

A Holistic Approach to Grid Management, Planning, and Operations

In an electric power environment that is highly distributed, decentralized, variable, and rapidly growing, Jain said there are two main challenges to improving the grid: handling load growth and integrating clean energy. Given the scale of these challenges and their impact on the wider ecosystem, he highlighted the need for a holistic approach to grid management, planning, and operations. He posited that siloing among these elements and across energy markets has impeded the ability to effectively address these issues and described how AI, a key driver of current load growth, can also help abate it through new tools that leverage AI, data integration, and software innovation.

To this end, Google X created Tapestry, a new, secure grid platform that enables cross-silo collaboration. Jain said that this end-to-end product approaches grid planning, management, and operations holistically to better leverage physical infrastructure and enable more effective planning. It uses modernized, AI-powered grid operations tools to integrate data on load and supply variability at the needed scale, speed, and granularity.

As an example of how collaborative AI–energy partnerships can implement coordinated solutions at scale, Jain described how a Tapestry pilot is helping Chile meet its ambitious decarbonization goals. Preliminary results show dramatically reduced computing time, more accurate weather predictions (critical for wind and solar generation), and an automated yet collaborative workflow, reducing the planning and operations burdens of load growth and clean energy integration. In response to a question, Jain noted that while the team has not explicitly modeled flexibility in terms of data center loads, they plan to extend the modeling to capture collaboration between data center owners and utilities. He added that there is a great deal of flexibility in terms of the parameters that are set up to capture demand, generation, planning, and optimization for different scenarios at different time horizons and granularities.

PANEL DISCUSSION

In an open discussion, panelists considered how the growth of AI data centers may intersect with other pressures that grid operators face, discussed the economics of energy and data center operations, and identified possible policy solutions that could help to advance progress and forestall some of the anticipated challenges.

Anticipating Growth

Panelists discussed different ways in which the expansion of AI data centers could impact the electric grid at national and local scales. Wilson asked panelists to comment on opportunities to address the impact of AI data centers on energy reliability, in light of the wide spikes and dips the grid can experience as AI processes cycle on and off. Samaras replied that the integration of data centers into the grid will be easier if AI algorithms can run more efficiently, smooth out the dips and spikes, and be responsive to price and valuation changes. Right now, data center owners are not sensitive to price, which suggests that a tariff that enables data centers to participate in demand response could help, but he emphasized the need to take a community-first approach in order to ensure that critical infrastructure, such as hospitals, can continue to access electricity that is affordable, reliable, clean, and resilient.

Wilson asked how to balance short-term operational opportunities with long-term investment goals. Roald replied that both are important, but that better integration and coordination between data centers and the grid in the short term is an important foundation for long-term investments. Roald also pointed out that business interests, more so than utilities, have driven power purchase agreements that have accelerated the clean energy transition. Unfortunately, grid constraints have created long interconnection queues and bottlenecks to integrating more renewable energy sources, which are growing in tandem with data center needs. To address this, she said that data centers need to create flexibilities that enable them to match their loads, regionally and hourly, with renewable power generation to further accelerate and leverage clean energy and avoid wasting it, which can happen if the grid is not able to absorb or distribute it.

When asked what makes today's large load increases different from those that utilities have faced in the past, Tsuchida replied that data centers are coming online that need power more quickly than utilities' traditional planning cycles allow for. He also noted that data on the total expected load amount is not enough—what is needed is a better understanding of the more granular and temporal energy needs so that utilities can direct resources more efficiently and cost effectively.

Wilson asked Jain if the tools he described could help to address some of these challenges. Jain replied that long interconnection queues exist because clean energy generation is a highly decentralized and variable two-way flow that is counter to how the grid was designed, creating a bottleneck impeding affordable, equitable, reliable energy. He expressed agreement with Tsuchida that traditional grid planning mechanisms and power sources are inadequate given the uncertainties, and he posited that AI-driven methods are necessary to help utilities address emerging challenges and plan with confidence at a higher level of granularity and accuracy.

Tsuchida added that incorporating flexible demand response into planning may depend on a utility's location and the willingness of system operators to pursue this approach. Wilson pointed out that some utilities are starting to incentivize flexibility by moving flexible sources to the front of their load interconnection queues. Roald expressed optimism about data center flexibilities and improved tools, models, and predictions to support grid operations, and said she hoped they would be widely adopted and fully leveraged to optimize the grid.

Julie Bolthouse, Piedmont Environmental Council, remarked that enormous data center growth in Northern Virginia has impacted state and local climate goals by increasing reliance on fossil fuel generation. She asked whether panelists envision a trajectory for AI that will ultimately plateau with some end amount of data generated (and energy needed) or whether the future will be more like a treadmill of unending growth. Tsuchida replied that as the cost of data storage goes down, it creates economies of scale and scope for data generation and use, but how much energy or data is needed ultimately depends on the consumers. Roald noted that efficiency improvements are helpful in keeping energy demands in check, but actual energy constraints would better incentivize data centers to minimize demand. Jain agreed that energy consumption is growing fast but speculated that it will plateau again—after an initial lag—when companies are incentivized to find efficiencies. As for data, he said that data generation will likely continue to accelerate, and since much of the data is of low quality, new software and AI techniques are needed to make better use of the data, especially for data relevant to improving grid planning and operation to meet energy and climate goals.

Benjamin Lee, University of Pennsylvania, asked if data centers were optimally sited. Tsuchida replied that from the perspective of data center owners, they are, because developers consider local factors—like energy rates, workforce potential, building costs, and weather—when siting their facilities. The siting of data centers creates more challenging issues for utilities, however, because they may need to build new generation or transmission capabilities and attempt to pass those costs onto data centers or all consumers, leading to complicated negotiations with multiple competing interests.

Cost, Market, and Supply Chain Issues

Ayse Coskun, Boston University, asked which energy market programs data centers could most easily join. Roald replied that there are a range of options for integrating with the grid, and the answer will depend on a data center's flexibility across workloads and timescales. Real-time ancillary markets, which pay for providing capacity, require minute-by-minute adjustments, while power envelopes enable participation in day-ahead markets. To facilitate participation in markets and make programs more accommodating to data centers, she noted that there is a need for a greater exchange of information between data centers and grid operators. Wilson added that European data centers are more involved in frequency regulation and participating in ancillary markets—markets that are currently less well defined in the United States.

Another participant pointed out that AI data centers have a very different balance of capital and operational expenditures than other types of data centers, such as those that support high-energy physics computation. Their capital expenditures are so high that operational costs like electricity essentially amounts to noise compared to hardware costs, which lessens the impact of ancillary service charges in influencing their decision-making. The participant asked if tariffs targeting AI data centers would be a more effective mechanism. Tsuchida replied that there are two tariff ideas—a new, all-inclusive tariff on AI data centers, or applying existing tariffs to AI data centers. He expressed his belief that the latter is more effective and avoids discrimination among customers, noting that some jurisdictions testing new tariffs are coming up against unresolved questions, such as who is charged, how long the tariff lasts, and how a data center can become part of the native load.

Samaras reiterated that the switch from AI training to inference has positive and negative grid impacts. As companies race to get ahead, an urgent request to bring a data center online would be less sensitive to price, so a tariff levied early on can help local utilities build more infrastructure. He also suggested that data centers could become more responsible grid participants by helping to accelerate the transition to cleaner power as overall electrification creates even more load demands. Systematic, deliberate, and ambitious use of AI can maximize benefits, minimize risks, and reduce emissions, but this vision will be off to a poor start if data centers are powered by diesel, natural gas, or other legacy fuels, he said.

Another participant noted that data center growth will impact not just the grid, but also its equipment suppliers, which are experiencing bottlenecks as demand skyrockets. AI data centers are being built by the world's largest companies, which are far larger financially than utilities and have very few price constraints; the participant pointed out that these companies could potentially vertically integrate suppliers, leading to unfair resource allocation. Wilson added that there is already a backlog of equipment supplies for the electric power grid, and regulated entities often cannot pay above a certain price without special approval. The issue of uncertainty also affects this dynamic, making investment decisions just as challenging for suppliers as for utilities and data centers. Tsuchida expressed his belief that the open market does eventually level out bottlenecks, equipment shortages, and high prices—sometimes with secondary markets and sometimes through new competitors—usually within a few years.

Policy Suggestions

Wilson asked panelists to highlight policy or research ideas that they view as important for making progress toward addressing challenges around the impacts of data centers on the grid. Samaras offered several suggestions to work toward a clean, affordable, reliable, and resilient grid. First, he expressed his support for continuing policies that ramp up nuclear power generation, along with advancing new policies to investigate geothermal power, leverage existing nuclear and hydropower capabilities, and advance long-duration energy storage and upgrades to reconductoring, transmission, and distribution infrastructure. He added that supply-chain challenges could be addressed with a policy compelling advanced market commitments or transmission expansion investments from developers, alongside community benefits agreements to ensure that critical infrastructure does not lose energy access. "Our existing system is built for both the temperature and the loads of the 20th century," he stated. "We have to rebuild that from scratch in a way that is digitally responsive to all these new loads."

Samaras also suggested that additional policy mechanisms could help to support the use of AI in enabling 100 GW of VPPs in the next decade to ensure that data center growth does not outpace grid capabilities while simultaneously demonstrating how AI can propel decarbonization goals. Finally, he underscored the need for better carbon accounting methods that enable industry to consider uncertainties, disclose their carbon footprints, and deliver more benefits to society.

Roald suggested advancing policies that incentivize data centers to participate in electricity markets and improve load flexibility. She noted that data centers are not merely reacting to price and carbon signals from the grid but contributing to them both in real time and over the long term, and incentives are needed to encourage them to be more active in grid orchestration. She also suggested that policies are needed to improve carbon accounting for real-time electricity, as current methods are ineffective and may actually increase emissions. If energy customers receive signals that reflect the physical reality of the grid's complex operations and suggest concrete actions, they can lower their own emissions and that of the grid as a whole.

Jain agreed with the other panelists' suggestions and recommended, as a short-term solution, a grid planning and operations policy to alleviate the clean energy interconnection bottleneck and enable more AI-driven efficiencies. To address inadequacies in the grid's digital architecture in the longer term, he said that a new digital architecture is needed to enable secure data sharing within and between companies and utilities and support more precise and auditable carbon accounting measures. He suggested that this new architecture should be decentralized, data-driven, and malleable—similar to the Internet.

Tsuchida suggested that the AI industry could lobby for a fair overall pricing structure that incentivizes data centers and utilities to make improvements in ways that are mutually beneficial. For example, he said that AI data center operators could do more to try to shrink their energy usage peaks, and creating a standard transmission charge could encourage grid operators and data centers to increase the adoption of renewables and grid-enhancing technologies.

SYSTEM OPERATOR PERSPECTIVES ON CONNECTING GRID-FRIENDLY DATA CENTERS

K. John Holmes, National Academies of Sciences, Engineering, and Medicine, moderated a discussion with Agee Springer of the Electric Reliability Council of Texas (ERCOT) and Robert Wright of Dominion Energy of Virginia. ERCOT is an independent system operator that maintains electric power reliability, ensures equitable interconnection access, and runs wholesale markets across most of Texas. Dominion is a traditional utility that serves residential and commercial customers, generates and transmits its own power, and participates in the wholesale electricity market. The discussion focused on current impacts of AI data centers, future opportunities, and the unknowns surrounding the interactions between AI data centers and the electric power grid.

Holmes noted that AI is at the leading edge of electricity growth as decarbonization strategies take hold. Wright said that AI has generated a lot of excitement in the electric power industry, which has historically been a relatively mundane industry. While AI is proving to be more complex and demanding than other challenges utilities have faced, it also presents unique opportunities to drive innovation and deliver safer, more reliable energy, such as from small nuclear reactors or long-duration energy storage. In addition, the incredibly fast growth of AI is driving innovation in other industries. Springer agreed that AI creates opportunities to make a positive change in the energy sector and the world. Based on current trends, he added that the supply, demand, and reliability challenges in 10 years will likely be very different from those seen today.

Wright stated that AI data center energy demands have the potential to both help and harm the grid. These data centers typically have very high loads that operate at peak capacity with few fluctuations, which is good for grid stability. However, data center load is highly sensitive to grid disturbances and can shut down, requiring major recovery operations for the customer. Data centers often have multiple redundancies to protect against these shutdowns, but as loads become more dense, they can also upset the balance between service and generation, another large challenge that needs to be addressed.

Springer echoed Wright's concerns. ERCOT is not synchronized with the rest of the U.S. grid and is much smaller. Data center demands represent only a small percentage of ERCOT's peak summer load, but they are very sensitive to grid disturbances, especially when they are clustered and still growing, like in Texas. These new loads, totaling an additional 5.5 GW of demand, are seeking immediate interconnection, and utilities are struggling to plan for and model them while maintaining day-to-day reliability and stability. Storms or load disruptions impact ERCOT's service-generation balance and could cause cascading outages. Springer emphasized the need to address these issues now through data center designs that prioritize grid stability and reliability and minimize grid overwhelm.

Building on Springer's remarks, Wright said that Virginia is also experiencing unprecedented demand and new interconnection requests. This has forced Dominion to innovate to maximize existing facilities' capabilities and improve outage scheduling processes to allow building new projects to maintain power reliability. In addition to making physical grid upgrades, Dominion is removing supply-chain constraints, employing new methods such as energized reconductoring, and improving customer transparency through service request platforms that share planning and process information, he said. Springer stated that ERCOT utilities are dealing with similar supply-chain, transmission, and workforce challenges. He said that the process that governs building new transmission lines is inadequate for today's fast-paced growth demands, because data center developers want to build where there is already adequate power. Holmes noted that rate payers also have a large role to play that is beyond the scope of this discussion but is fundamental to the electric power system.

Holmes asked if ERCOT or Dominion had experienced demand fluctuations during AI training. Springer replied that ERCOT suspects but has not yet confirmed this and sees these fluctuations as a growing concern. He posited that it may be possible to coordinate load fluctuations with grid operations to avoid disrupting stability or reliability, benefiting everyone.

Wright noted that unknowns around AI's training and inference process variabilities make predicting grid impacts challenging. To enable a better understanding of these fluctuations, he suggested that utilities and data centers should share data to improve coordination, predict impacts, and understand needed response. He also suggested that training centers may need to be located separately from inference centers, given that their energy needs are different. Springer agreed that grid impacts from AI fluctuations are challenging to predict and more data is needed. "Every layer we peel back, at least in the ERCOT region, we keep finding five more questions underneath every one that we answer," he stated. "So, I think understanding is really going to be important for those of us charged with reliability."

5

Sustainability Analysis of Data Centers

Eric Masanet, University of California, Santa Barbara, moderated a panel discussion focusing on the environmental and social repercussions of artificial intelligence (AI) data centers, both locally through land, water, and energy demands as well as globally from increased emissions, supply-chain impacts, and pollutants generated throughout the life cycle of data center equipment and infrastructure. The panelists were Davide D'Ambrosio, International Energy Agency (IEA); Julie Bolthouse, Piedmont Environmental Council; Laura Gonzalez Guerrero, Clean Virginia; Sarah Boyd, Aligned Incentives; and Cooper Elsworth, Google.

PANELIST REMARKS

Data Center Electricity Demand Growth

D'Ambrosio shared IEA findings regarding the current and future energy demands of data centers. While data centers account for a relatively small part of the overall projected growth in electricity demand through 2030 (Figure 5-1), they are growing fast globally and nationally, and investment in them has outpaced clean energy investment.[1] Compared to other types of industry facilities like steel plants, factories, mines, and even warehouses, data centers also show a high tendency to

[1] International Energy Agency (IEA), 2024, *World Energy Outlook 2024,* IEA Publications, https://www.iea.org/reports/world-energy-outlook-2024.

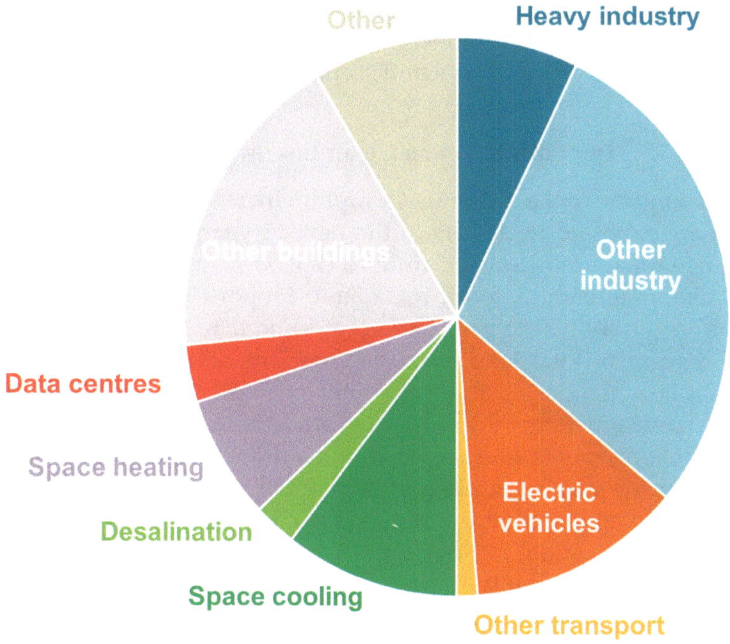

FIGURE 5-1 Electricity demand for 2030, reflecting scenario results based on the International Energy Agency (IEA) Stated Policies Scenario.
NOTE: See https://www.iea.org/reports/global-energy-and-climate-model/stated-policies-scenario-steps and https://www.iea.org/reports/global-energy-and-climate-model/understanding-gec-model-scenarios.
SOURCE: Davide D'Ambrosio, IEA, presentation to the workshop, November 12, 2024. CC BY 4.0.

cluster in the same geographic areas. This clustering is driven by a need for data centers to be located close to available infrastructure, power supply, customers, and workforce; however, it also creates strains on local communities and utilities.

D'Ambrosio emphasized that numerous sources of uncertainty around data and AI deployment, technological advances, and efficiency improvements impede the ability to accurately project U.S. data center energy demands, adding that much of this uncertainty stems from a lack of clear reporting on data centers' current energy use and operating characteristics, requiring modelers to make assumptions.[2,3,4,5,6,7] Given these uncertainties, D'Ambrosio recommended caution when modeling and using sensitivity analyses and scenario-based approaches.

Impediments to a Clean Energy Transition

Responding to the challenge of rapidly increasing energy demands—which are expected to double in the next 15 years[8]—creates a daunting challenge for investor-owned utilities (IOUs) such as Dominion Energy. Data centers already account for a large proportion of total load in the state of Virginia—a little over 20 percent—and that is projected to increase to 55 percent of total load by 2039. Guerrero described how, despite a Virginia law mandating the retirement of fossil fuel plants, Dominion Energy has claimed that the only way to meet the coming load is by delaying plant retirements and increasing gas-fired generation, a significant setback for the state's path to curtailing greenhouse gas emissions.

One challenge is that the regulatory cost-of-service model followed by IOUs is inadequate to price data center demand, Guerrero said. This outdated compensation framework maximizes profits through increased capital expenditures to increase the base rate and generate more shareholder revenue, inadvertently disincentivizing cleaner, more responsible, and more cost-effective ways to manage growth. Residents would see a

---

[2] J. Albers, V. Dahiya, A. Fraym, and J. Howe, 2024, *2024 Global Data Center Market Comparison*, Cushman & Wakefield, https://www.cushmanwakefield.com/en/insights/global-data-center-market-comparison.

[3] L. Greden, O. Yashkova, R. Brothers, S. Graham, n.d., *Datacenter Trends: Sustainable Datacenter Builds and CO_2 Emissions*, https://www.idc.com/getdoc.jsp?containerId=IDC_P33186, accessed December 15, 2024.

[4] A. Green, H. Tai, J. Noffsinger, P. Sachdeva, A. Bhan, and R. Sharma, 2024, "How Data Centers and the Energy Sector Can Sate AI's Hunger for Power," *McKinsey & Company* (blog), September 17, https://www.mckinsey.com/industries/private-capital/our-insights/how-data-centers-and-the-energy-sector-can-sate-ais-hunger-for-power.

[5] Mordor Intelligence, n.d., "Data Center Market Size & Share Analysis - Growth Trends & Forecasts Up to 2030," https://www.mordorintelligence.com/industry-reports/data-center-colocation-market, accessed December 15, 2024.

[6] D. Patel, J.E. Ontiveros, and D. Nishball, 2024, "Datacenter Anatomy Part 1: Electrical Systems," *Semi Analysis* (blog), October 14, https://semianalysis.com/2024/10/14/datacenter-anatomy-part-1-electrical.

[7] E. Masanet, N. Lei, and J. Koomey, 2024, "To Better Understand AI's Growing Energy Use, Analysts Need a Data Revolution," *Joule* 8(9):2427–2436, https://doi.org/10.1016/j.joule.2024.07.018.

[8] V.B. Link, 2024, "Commonwealth of Virginia, Ex Rel. State Corporation Commission, In Re: Virginia Electric and Power Company's 2024 Integrated Resource Plan Filing Pursuant to Va. Code § 56-597 et Seq. Case No. PUR-2024-00184," sent October 15, https://cdn-dominionenergy-prd-001.azureedge.net/-/media/pdfs/global/company/irp/2024-irp-w_o-appendices.pdf?rev=c03a36c512024003ae9606a6b6a239f3.

much lower energy bill in 15 years if IOUs included load growth in their ratepayer cost calculations.

Community Impacts of Data Center Growth

Building on Guerrero's comments, Bolthouse discussed how Piedmont Environmental Council has sought to understand the impacts of data centers on communities in Northern Virginia, which is home to the largest concentration of AI data centers in the world. The organization focuses on Virginia's Loudoun, Albemarle, and Clark counties with a mission to protect and restore the area's lands and waters, improve air quality, and build more sustainable communities. She described how the rapid growth of data centers in this area threatens decades of conservation efforts and undermines Virginia's clean energy and climate goals.[9,10]

Bolthouse said that the first data centers to come to the area were built far away from protected areas and brought jobs and revenue to the community. However, as more and more energy-hungry data centers have come online, negative impacts for the surrounding communities have begun to accumulate and spread far beyond the data center locations themselves. The utilities claim that they have an obligation to provide power to customers, but she said that in reality this means they are offering power they cannot provide (Figure 5-2).[11] Bolthouse also noted that the service agreements that utilities enter into with data centers lack state oversight or consideration of impacts to ratepayers. "All this is happening behind closed doors, so there's really not that much transparency around it," she stated.

In practice, electric utilities' obligation to provide service to anyone who requests it within their service territory, combined with the rapid growth in customer contracts, has created a crisis that utilities say can only be solved through a return to gas-fired generation, in conflict with Virginia's laws and decarbonization goals. In addition to spurring continued, and even increased, fossil fuel use—through the delayed retirement of coal facilities

---

[9] Piedmont Environmental Council, n.d., "Existing and Proposed Data Centers—A Web Map," https://www.pecva.org/work/energy-work/data-centers/existing-and-proposed-data-centers-a-web-map, accessed April 21, 2025.

[10] J. Albers, V. Dahiya, A. Fraym, and J. Howe, 2024, *2024 Global Data Center Market Comparison*, Cushman & Wakefield, https://www.cushmanwakefield.com/en/insights/global-data-center-market-comparison.

[11] V.B. Link, 2024, "Commonwealth of Virginia, Ex Rel. State Corporation Commission, In Re: Virginia Electric and Power Company's 2024 Integrated Resource Plan Filing Pursuant to Va. Code § 56-597 et Seq. Case No. PUR-2024-00184," sent October 15, https://cdn-dominionenergy-prd-001.azureedge.net/-/media/pdfs/global/company/irp/2024-irp-w_o-appendices.pdf?rev=c03a36c512024003ae9606a6b6a239f3.

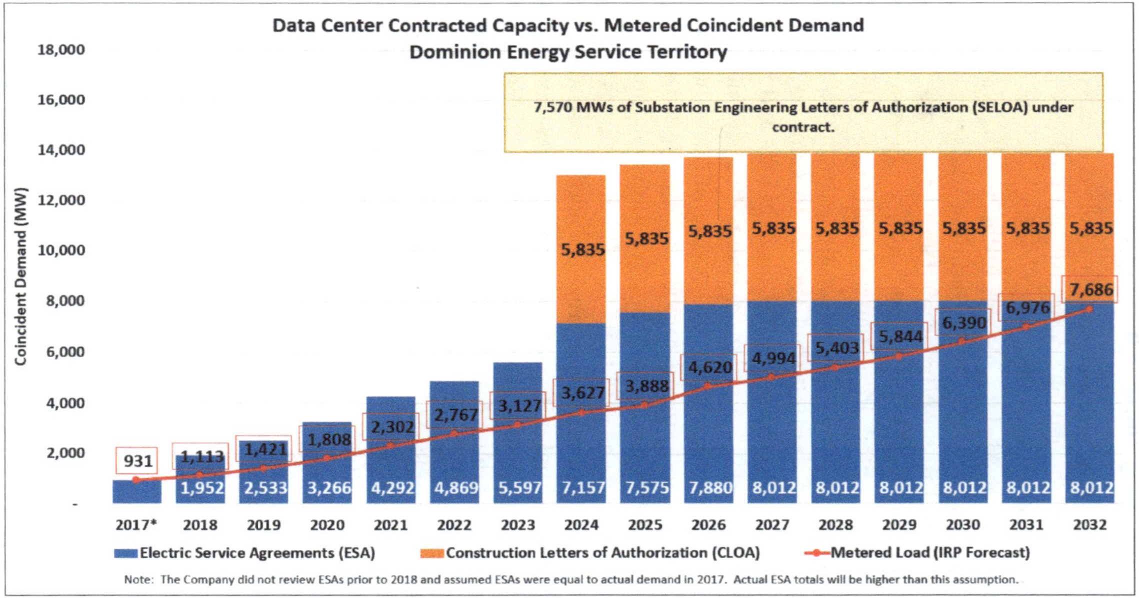

FIGURE 5-2 Projected data center contracted capacity versus metered coincident demand in Dominion Energy service territory.
SOURCE: Julie Bolthouse, Piedmont Environmental Council, presentation to the workshop, November 12, 2024.

and the approval of more than 4,000 diesel-powered generators permitted as backup power—Bolthouse added that the water demands of data centers also pose a threat to communities and ecosystems. For example, Loudoun Water reported a 250 percent increase in potable water consumption from data centers between 2020–2024, with the amount of potable water used by data centers now surpassing reclaimed water.

Accounting for Cradle-to-Gate Emissions for Artificial Intelligence Equipment

Boyd discussed the emissions impacts connected with data center expansion that are embodied in data center equipment and occur before a data center even becomes operational. If the infrastructure and computing equipment necessary to build data centers—integrated circuits, semiconductors, cabling, processing units, memory, and more—were manufactured with renewable energy, their overall life-cycle emissions would be dramatically lower. While strides have been made to reduce these "cradle-to-gate" emissions, AI data centers are projected to create an additional 20–50 metric tons of carbon dioxide by 2030 under a business-as-usual scenario for the production of storage wafers, memory wafers, and processor wafers.[12]

Boyd said that technical solutions are needed to better understand and reduce carbon emissions during manufacturing and operations, along with policy incentives to encourage the adoption of these solutions. In the near term, she highlighted the need to increase the ability to meet supply-chain and production demands for renewable sources of energy, while using effective fluorinated emissions abatement strategies to reduce greenhouse gas emissions generated during certain manufacturing processes. In the medium term, she said that research is needed to advance alternative process chemistries and to develop more advanced fluorinated greenhouse gas emission abatement strategies. In the long term, she said that it will be important to optimize every part of the AI data center supply chain for minimal emissions. She added that innovative work is being done at the Interuniversity Microelectronics Centre (IMEC), and that IMEC is a close collaborator with the National Institute of Standards and Technology (NIST).

These challenges are complex, involve multiple actors and fast-changing industries, and will require collaboration to create incentives and

[12] O. Burkacky, M. Pototzky, D. Tang, and W. Zhu, 2024, "Generative AI: The Next S-Curve for the Semiconductor Industry?" *McKinsey & Company*, March 29, https://www.mckinsey.com/industries/semiconductors/our-insights/generative-ai-the-next-s-curve-for-the-semiconductor-industry.

drive action. Boyd pointed to two policies from Europe that can serve as models: the Corporate Sustainability Due Diligence Directive (CSDDD) and the Ecodesign for Sustainable Products (ESPR) Directive. The CSDDD ensures that companies have climate transition plans that address their value chain and 5-year detailed action plans that target achievement and penalize failure. The ESPR sets incentives and drives action through tracking products' sustainability attributes.

Corporate Sustainability Commitments

Elsworth discussed the role of corporate commitments in advancing sustainability for AI data centers, highlighting the commitments made by Google and the strategies the company is employing to achieve them. Google has committed to ambitious sustainability goals to decarbonize the company's operations. This includes reducing absolute emissions by 50 percent by 2030 from a 2019 baseline, sourcing carbon removals to neutralize remaining emissions, and running all data centers on carbon-free energy 24 hours a day, 7 days a week. The rapid growth of AI data centers has posed a new challenge in achieving these targets; however, and the company is focused on advancing AI innovation without contributing to emissions growth.

To that end, Elsworth said that an important first step is to create tools that can gather more granular emissions data from data centers, enabling users to make informed decisions that minimize emissions. Action-focused emissions data will help companies understand that emissions can be broken down by workloads, AI models, customers, and products; enable the creation of carbon-aware computing optimizations that reduce specific workloads' emissions; and match hourly workloads with clean energy availability to ensure the grid supports demand.

To support this, Google created an hourly carbon emissions monitoring tool that breaks down emissions by individual workload and location. This helps to shed light on energy supply and demand and enable the use of modeling tools to identify opportunities to make workloads more carbon-efficient, decoupling energy growth from emissions growth. For example, Google's data centers now work harder when solar or wind generation is strongest. Cloud customers can also access these tools to maximize decarbonization.

While achieving this level of granularity has been challenging given a general lack of consensus on methods to measure AI emissions, Elsworth said that the company is confident that the tools will help to reduce data center emissions. He added that efforts are underway to improve methods to collect the granular data needed to verify that data center processes are using carbon-free energy.

PANEL DISCUSSION

In an open discussion, panelists considered a variety of issues around the impacts of data centers on energy costs and emissions, the responsibilities of different stakeholders, and the importance of addressing uncertainties. They concluded by naming what they see as key sustainability challenges along with possible research directions or policy solutions to address them.

Energy Costs and Responsibilities

Paige Wesselink, Sierra Club, said that in her view, it seems unfair that the high concentration of data centers in Northern Virginia means that a single utility (Dominion Energy) and its customers are bearing the burden of handling approximately 70 percent of the world's Internet traffic.[13] Bolthouse agreed that many of the costs associated with data center expansion ultimately wind up being unfairly subsidized by the public. Even though AI is not yet a marketable product, the infrastructure being rapidly built for it is bringing huge costs to utilities, customers' energy bills, the environment, and public health.

Guerrero agreed, adding that utilities are not incentivized to change their business model or question data centers' energy demands, which leaves other customers and communities to shoulder the burdens while the AI industry will ultimately reap the benefits. "How do we make sure that the costs are correctly allocated to those companies that are set to profit the most out of it and make sure that we avoid placing the risk on residential customers that are suffering the burden not only of the cost but of the natural gas facilities, the coal plants, the water issues—all the things we talked about today?" Guerrero asked. "It's a philosophical question about who is paying and who should pay."

Arman Shehabi, Lawrence Berkeley National Laboratory, asked panelists to comment on why utilities do not pass on the costs of building more capacity to data centers. Bolthouse replied that IOUs make profits from new capital expenditures and also claim they cannot satisfy contract deadlines without using legacy fossil-fuel energy sources. In one case, she said that Virginia's State Corporation Commission did not require a data center developer to pay for anything more than distribution for energy delivery, setting a precedent that new transmission lines in Northern Virginia be paid for by ratepayers. She also noted that the Data Center Coalition is a powerful lobby and said that new policies are needed to protect the public interest.

---

[13] Northern Virginia Regional Commission, n.d., "Data Centers," https://www.novaregion.org/1598/Data-Centers, accessed April 21, 2025.

Guerrero noted that the commission is considering charging data centers directly for new transmission lines, but developers are fighting it by arguing that that plan is discriminatory. She said that this is in line with a general pattern she sees in which industry initially expresses a willingness to pay for costs associated with their activities, but then when it comes to regulatory proceedings, they "fight tooth and nail" against paying. She praised Google for its transparency and commitment to sustainability, but expressed frustration with other companies and industry associations regarding this behavior.

Masanet asked Guerrero to explain more about what she sees as the impacts on ratepayers and suggested that energy economists could help inform solutions. Guerrero reiterated that utilities make money through capital expenditures and said that they will need new incentives if they are to align maximizing least-cost alternatives with data center demand flexibility—an approach that is rarely considered or reflected in utilities' resource plans. In addition, she said that stakeholders need to encourage utilities to model different scenarios to account for load forecast uncertainties and avoid relying on traditional, fossil fuel–based infrastructure. The key challenge is to provide reliable power for this uncertain load without over- or under-building. She also said that ratepayers need to be protected from early-cost-recovery schemes that increase the public's energy rates to cover investments before they are used and useful, a practice that she said has harmed consumers in South Carolina and Florida.

Elsworth suggested that data centers could break down the use of cloud services by customer and product to understand the value created by different sets of AI models and tools and potentially create separate prices for different models, noting that this approach could yield fairer pricing models as opposed to a blanket price that aggregates all data center operations.

Accounting for Environmental Impacts

Panelists discussed different approaches to understanding and addressing the environmental impacts of data center expansion. Wesselink noted that companies can claim net-zero status not only by making their data center operations emissions-free but by purchasing carbon offsets in a different region, away from the impacts they cause locally. As a result, companies may be able to claim they are supporting sustainability even as they create adverse environmental impacts in certain places. Elsworth acknowledged that the definition of net-zero can be massaged, but Google's overall goals, to reduce emissions and support high-quality carbon removal, can be achieved by closing loopholes in carbon accounting and improving standards to ensure local and hourly matching of carbon-free loads. Bolthouse added that regulatory oversight is needed to require transparency and ensure a level playing field in accounting for carbon emissions.

Masanet asked Bolthouse to expand on the local impacts of data center clusters. She replied that communities have some agency in solving these issues—for example, with local land use decisions. However, while the impacts of data centers to air quality, water supply, and electricity rates are felt on a regional scale, the decision makers who set policies and grant permits are focused on the local scale, are incentivized to consider revenue and tax benefits, and are not responsible for meeting state regulations. She suggested a need for more transparency and oversight at the state level so that local decision makers are better able to understand regional impacts and react to harms when utilities and data centers move too quickly with minimal supervision. For example, she said that the rush to develop data centers and expand electricity infrastructure to meet their energy demands has resulted in cemeteries being destroyed, water quality being adversely affected, and transmission lines being routed through protected areas, recreational space, and private property.

Andrew Chien, University of Chicago, asked if building infrastructure-intensive super-campuses to attract data centers would be one possible approach to minimize local impacts. Bolthouse replied that it might work in new locations, but the overall pressure on the grid is so large that creating all of that power and building new transmission lines—or even a small nuclear reactor—is an enormous challenge. Guerrero agreed that this may be a solution to one problem, but who pays for the increased cost of power is still unresolved.

Masanet asked Elsworth how AI industry stakeholders can help to drive the decoupling of AI and emissions. He replied that energy is the link between the two, and data centers present an opportunity to test decarbonization methods on a global scale. He said that careful data collection will be essential to informing efforts to decouple energy from AI performance and to decouple energy from emissions. For decoupling energy from AI performance, he noted that Google designed a full-stack data center using more efficient hardware, software, and models, improving energy efficiency by 1.5-fold. Moving data centers into the cloud will also improve energy efficiency. For decoupling the energy used for AI data centers from emissions, he said that each data center action or component must be disaggregated and monitored to optimize workloads for minimal emissions. In addition, he said that incentives are needed to push for carbon-aware data center siting and clean energy procurement to enable data centers to influence the grid hourly and bring more renewable energy online.

Boyd noted that in addition to carbon emissions, the manufacturing of semiconductor chips has high water demands. Factories' water needs often constrain the local supply, making it important to site fabrication facilities ("fabs") with consideration of water availability. In addition, while fabs have waste abatement or treatment facilities, some pollutants are more challenging to abate. She said that research is under way to develop replacements or effective waste treatment for perfluoroalkyl substances (PFASs), a class of substances used in manufacturing processes across many sectors, which have very extended longevity in the environment. Substitution of PFAS is a major challenge, given the many applications of PFAS-containing materials in fabrication, and will take many years to accomplish.

Addressing Uncertainty

Masanet asked D'Ambrosio how the IEA views and communicates the large amount of uncertainty around data center expansion, energy, and sustainability. D'Ambrosio highlighted many sources of uncertainty that make it hard to predict data centers' future energy needs. For example, efficiency gains in hardware and software could inadvertently drive-up electricity demand—this is known as Jevons paradox, the idea that increasing efficiency leads to higher overall consumption rather than savings. Jevons paradox is disputed in the AI community. Different economic and technological contexts, actual trends in AI adoption, shifts in AI workloads to edge devices, and sustainability efforts will all affect whether Jevons paradox will hold true. Another source of uncertainty is related to policies that lead to trade restrictions on key components and associated constraints in chip production, infrastructure, grid capacity, power generation, and permitting. The IEA, as a neutral actor, is convening a collaborative, multi-stakeholder conference to discuss these issues,[14,15] aggregate critical information, share data securely, and identify solutions. Masanet agreed that such a collaboration could greatly reduce uncertainty. However, he cautioned that more data sharing is needed before analysts can fully understand the current picture and improve models to enable more accurate predictions.

Sustainability Challenges and Solutions

To close the discussion, Masanet asked each panelist to name what they see as a key sustainability challenge along with research or policy opportunities that could advance solutions.

---

[14] IEA, n.d., "Global Conference on Energy & AI," https://www.iea.org/events/global-conference-on-energy-ai#overview, accessed April 21, 2025.

[15] IEA, 2024, "Chair's Summary of the High-Level Roundtable on Energy & AI," December 5, https://www.iea.org/news/chair-s-summary-of-the-high-level-roundtable-on-energy-and-ai.

Suggesting that carbon impacts would become another parameter that influences the commercial readiness of semiconductor research, Boyd posited that programs of the CHIPS and Science Act of 2022 and other semiconductor research grants under NIST should require evaluations similar to IMEC's addressing the carbon impacts of semiconductor processing and architectures early in development.

D'Ambrosio highlighted the need for greater transparency around data centers' operations in order to more fully understand the granular energy demands and the factors that influence them, from server configurations and network and storage capacity to training and inference. Building on this point, Elsworth underscored the need for stronger monitoring and accounting standards to de-risk the growth of AI. He noted that other industries have faced similar inflection periods and built pre-competitive relationships to collaboratively redefine standards and create methods to disclose emissions that work for all stakeholders.

Bolthouse advocated for greater regulatory oversight to enforce transparency around data centers' energy and water use. She also added that there is a need for more research to understand the potential air quality impacts from onsite generation at data centers, especially in areas where data centers are highly concentrated. Guerrero highlighted the need for more research into cost allocation. If electricity were more fairly and correctly priced, she suggested, this could drive down demand. AI services today seem free and harmless to use, but in part this is because people do not realize their true costs. "There is a gas plant built in a county in Virginia that is mostly populated by Black communities, Hispanic communities, and low-income communities—and there is a direct link between every time we [use] ChatGPT and how much emissions this gas line is producing," she said.

6

Societal Considerations of Data Center Expansion

Data center expansion can affect economies and communities through impacts on energy consumption, the environment, and workforces. Prashant Shenoy, University of Massachusetts Amherst, moderated a panel that explored impacts of the expansion of artificial intelligence (AI) data centers for local communities, society more broadly, and the global environment, as well as policies and regulations to address these impacts. The panelists were Kelly Sanders, University of Southern California; Nate Benforado; Southern Environmental Law Center; Tim Cywinski, Sierra Club; and Varun Rai, University of Texas at Austin.

PANELIST REMARKS

Approaching Artificial Intelligence Concerns as a Catalyst for Progress

Sanders posited that the need to address issues around the expansion of AI data centers could be leveraged as a catalyst to spur progress toward decarbonization and other goals as the United States charts the future of its electric power grid. The grid is the backbone of the physical economy, while AI is becoming the backbone of the digital economy, and both are critical to modern life. Where they intersect, issues of national security, global competition, geopolitics, and decarbonization arise. While the growth of AI and its related energy demands has potential negative consequences, Sanders highlighted how the current moment also offers unique opportunities to create policy solutions with broader impacts.

Echoing a point made by other speakers throughout the workshop, Sanders noted that data center energy demands are important and growing but still are anticipated to represent only a relatively small portion of the rapidly increasing demands on the U.S. grid driven by vehicle and building electrification, hydrogen production, and other factors over the next few decades. To meet future demands, raise grid capacity, and achieve decarbonization goals, she underscored the need for technology companies, utilities, policy makers, and other stakeholders to create equitable, effective policies that protect ratepayers and minimize health and environmental hazards. However, it takes more than good ideas to create policy, Sanders said, noting that policies are connected with time and space. To make the most of this moment in which there is a great deal of attention focused on AI and its future, she suggested finding ways to connect policies around AI and technology with other goals for the grid more broadly. "We could look at this issue like the sky is falling, but I really challenge us to say, we're going to meet the moment and we're going to pull through decarbonization and all of these other societal priorities as we think about this issue," Sanders said.

Increasing Transparency in Decision-Making

Benforado highlighted the importance of transparency in informing smart decisions around data center expansions and their interactions with the electric power grid. Given the potentially large impacts that data centers have on land, water, and energy needs both locally and globally, he emphasized that local utilities and officials need more information about these impacts to make intelligent decisions and plan for the future amid unprecedented growth and uncertainty.

Data center operators negotiate in private with localities and utilities for zoning approval and service agreements. Utilities today are using those agreements to amend their plans and justify new fossil fuel–based infrastructure, which generates profits but deprioritizes climate goals. In Virginia, two main utilities have what is essentially a monopoly in their service areas, and regulatory oversight merely requires reliable power at a fair price. In addition to posing a setback for decarbonization goals, Benforado noted that this situation could result in an overbuilt grid if planned data centers do not materialize or AI fails to become commercially viable, leaving local customers footing large bills.

Benforado posited that it is possible to create a more sustainable path that supports AI data center growth without sacrificing decarbonization goals. To achieve this, he underscored the need for more transparent negotiations; more coordination at the local, state, and regional levels; and more collaboration among utilities, regulators, and other stakeholders to make informed decisions that mitigate uncertainties, maintain reliability, and prioritize clean energy strategies such as storage, offshore wind, and grid-enhancing technologies.

The Urgency of Action to Protect Public Interests

Cywinski outlined an urgent need for strong policies to combat AI data centers' power demands, which he said unfairly threaten climate goals and raise consumer electricity rates. As examples of the negative impacts AI data centers can have on local communities, he said that water-hungry AI campuses are being built in rural areas that are already struggling with drought, while new utility infrastructure is worsening air quality in economically disadvantaged areas. In addition to these environmental impacts, he said that data center expansion is exacerbating rate increases, creating serious economic strains, especially in places like Virginia where 29 percent of residents already report forgoing basic necessities to pay their electric bills.

Cywinski said that the United States can be an AI leader while minimizing harm to the public and the environment. To do so, however, will require overcoming unfair structures that support data center growth at the expense of protecting communities and the environment, policy lags that allow for growth to continue unchecked while protective policies are being formulated, and a dearth of transparency into data centers' needs and operations. While there are promising technological solutions, he said that time is running out to craft effective policy and protect public interests.

Opportunities and Challenges in Transforming the Electric Industry

Rai highlighted key opportunities and challenges AI data centers bring during a pivotal moment for the electric power industry. He said that AI can enable enormous change, not just in the electricity market but across the entire economy and society, but the challenges of meeting the demands of AI data centers are markedly different from those associated with the types of load increases that drove grid expansions in the past.

Rai posited that these large and variable loads present opportunities to transform the electric industry, utility business models, and regulations, as well as an opportunity to push technology companies toward electrification. For example, innovations in grid technology and mechanical and electrical engineering will be needed to enable data centers to dynamically interact with the grid. In addition, he suggested that radical changes will be needed to update the utility sector's approaches to regulation, infrastructure investments, cost recovery, rate design, load integration, and more. He added that AI can also drive behind-the-meter changes to enable better grid integration.

There are also many challenges, many of which arise from uncertainties with regard to the scale, timeline, and location of data centers, as well as uncertainties about when and how AI will be commercially viable. To plan amid these uncertainties, he underscored the need for a multistakeholder collaboration that encourages experimentation, innovation, flexibility, and diversity. Another challenge is the lack of adequate renewable energy generation and storage, which has led to a need for more natural gas generation in order to meet growing demands. However, he posited that even that challenge can be seen as an opportunity to clean up the natural gas production process and minimize associated emissions.

PANEL DISCUSSION

In an open discussion, panelists delved deeper into data center impacts, strategies for driving change through policy, AI challenges and opportunities, and increasing electrification.

Data Center Impacts

Andrew Grimshaw, Lancium, expressed his concern about Virginia's approach to data centers and the impacts they are having in the state. He stated that it is important to separate AI's impacts on society from data centers' impacts, and he posited that data centers should be built where there is more access to renewable power and storage and more land to build these resources out—places like rural Texas, not Virginia. Cywinski agreed, noting that he is also opposed to what he characterized as "reckless" data center development in places like Virginia. Despite the economic and environmental drawbacks for communities, projects are still being approved and serviced through increases in fossil fuel generation. He argued that this situation is both environmentally irresponsible and unfair to Virginia's taxpayers, but it is the easiest solution for utilities and promises them large profits.

To address this disconnect, Cywinski suggested that AI companies should pay more of the energy and infrastructure costs associated with data center expansion. He noted that technology companies have overpromised and under-delivered before, and he said that it is unfair for local communities to pay for new utility infrastructure that brings a plethora of problems, including excess construction noise, more transmission lines, increased bills, and decreased air and water quality. "We're subsidizing them through taxpayer money. We are giving them extremely luxurious tax benefits. And then we have to pay for the new power plants through our monthly electric bills," he stated. "Is this the price of progress in technology ... that a group of people in one state or a collection of states have to pay for the benefit for the rest of us?"

Jonathan Herz, Environmental and Energy Study Institute, wondered if economic analyses of data center builds included cogeneration potential or external costs like energy. Benforado replied that their economic analyses are not made public; data centers file needs and projections with utility commissions, but the process moves too fast, and the terms are subject to very little oversight. In addition, he said that data centers and utilities are so fragmented that it is challenging to conduct holistic evaluations to understand and optimize or mitigate their cumulative impacts on the grid, communities, and the world.

Rai highlighted the value of more widely communicating the environmental impacts of AI data centers to increase public awareness of these issues. He also suggested that data centers could create a model of shared responsibility and accountability through increased transparency, data sharing, community engagement, and commitments to self-regulated decarbonization goals. Simply modeling data center demand does not always capture the full picture; instead, he posited that researchers should more carefully examine these demands to better coordinate the dynamic and growing drivers of AI across sectors. He reiterated that in the short-term, AI data center growth will require increased natural gas production, which is unfortunate but does create opportunities to experiment with new approaches.

Benjamin Lee, University of Pennsylvania, asked if carbon-free voluntary pledges had any impact on decreasing data center emissions or advancing clean energy generation. Sanders replied that emissions are challenging to evaluate and there is a lack of standardization around how to define "100 percent clean energy." However, she said that many large companies do appear to be concerned about their emissions profiles and suggested that more rigorous definitions and standards could help to advance meaningful progress. Rai added that hourly matching can advance clean energy generation and there has been progress on this front, but the growth is simply happening too quickly for renewable generation to keep up. Companies may make carbon-free pledges or pay more for power purchase agreements, but if they do not directly influence actual energy generation, utilities may often wind up using fossil fuel–based generation to meet the demand anyway. As a result, Rai said, "the rest of the system gets browner while the commitments get greener."

Building on this point, Cywinski said that in an ideal world, data center growth would pause until the benefits and harms could be more accurately weighed at the local and global levels to inform responsible decision-making. Unfortunately, that is unrealistic—AI is not slowing down, pointing to an urgent need for safeguards to encourage responsible growth. Creating such safeguards, however, will require massive political will, something that in turn requires public education, influence, and representation to create a better-informed citizenry that can move policy forward, he said.

Driving Change with Policy

Panelists discussed how policies on the part of governments, utilities, and technology companies can help to address concerns and drive change. Andrew Chien, University of Chicago, noted that data centers are at the intersection of a patchwork of municipal, regional, and state regulations and policies that weigh benefits and trade-offs differently. Cywinski agreed, stating that the lack of uniformity among regulations and safeguards enables large companies to influence local decisions and obscure potentially negative impacts. Greater harmonization around regulations and policies could force them to at least consider, if not prioritize, energy efficiency and public health issues, but right now policy lags behind the industry and technological advances, adding to the urgency of the problem.

Benforado suggested that it would be very powerful if data centers united around decarbonization goals and advocated for better regulation at the state, local, and utility-commission levels. Cywinski agreed, noting that in his experience, industry interests can move quickly to influence and accomplish policy goals. He suggested that the technology industry should use its influence to uphold public climate commitments, advocate for clean energy policies, and oppose increased fossil fuel production as a way to meet data centers' energy demands. Sanders also pointed out that some localities are relaxing air and water quality restrictions to attract data centers—for example, allowing large deployments of diesel-powered backup generators—and stressed the need to advocate against decisions like these that allow data center expansion to worsen pollution in local communities.

Rai agreed that policy goals are important but noted that policies often change when administrations change. However, even though a new administration could deprioritize clean energy policy or innovative financial incentives, he posited that it is still possible to better align the current patchwork of state and federal regulations through consumer and activist-led engagement focused around increasing data sharing and transparency and holding utilities and technology companies accountable for their commitments and actions. Benforado shared that there are bright spots; for example, some states are passing new regulations or even banning data centers, and others are experimenting with de-risking mechanisms, such as preferential systems or interruptible contracts, to protect existing customers. He also said that innovative pricing structures that incentivize data centers to choose between renewable or fossil fuel–based energy or implement demand response mechanisms during peak load times could have a large impact.

Chien noted that another challenge is that stakeholders have to make important decisions amid great uncertainty. One way to tip the scales in favor of clean energy generation over fossil fuels—in line with public goals and, in many cases, legal mandates—is to alter cost recovery rules to drive decisions in the direction of decarbonization. Sanders agreed that policy tools such as financial incentives, loan guarantees, and other de-risking mechanisms have successfully increased the appeal of emerging technologies. She added that policies that make incumbent strategies less attractive are also needed to encourage utilities to consider alternatives to building more fossil fuel–based infrastructure. Utilities are used to "perverse economics" that essentially incentivize the building of capital-intensive projects, which can come at the expense of more clean and economical options like energy efficiency, demand-side management, and clean energy sources. Cywinski agreed, noting that creating these mechanisms can be easier than passing policies, especially when what is popular and what is possible are not in alignment. In addition, it can be especially challenging to make gains on policy when industry has a strong influence over legislation, which he said is often the case with utilities.

Artificial Intelligence Challenges and Opportunities

Shenoy asked the panelists to elaborate on the challenges and opportunities they see with AI. Sanders agreed that AI presents opportunities to transform society and drive clean energy, but these benefits could also come at great costs. Utilities are arguing that they can only meet today's increased demand with an increase in natural gas investment, forgoing decarbonization strategies. She said that utility customers should be a part of these conversations. There are already efforts from large load customers interested in having more opportunities to buy clean energy to band together and pressure utilities to choose more clean energy pathways going forward. However, there is also the risk that buyers can unite and lobby for their interests through processes that are opaque to the public. "We have this catalyzing moment," she stated. "Do we use this to move fast toward a decarbonized future … or do we use this moment as an opportunity to backtrack into natural gas?"

Rai agreed that AI has tremendous potential value, and meeting its energy demands—whether through renewable energy or fossil fuel generation—will have local and global impacts. He said that community perspectives and increased data sharing should be integrated into early-stage discussions to improve transparency, create a more holistic picture of the impacts, and avoid regrettable decisions. If AI is wildly successful, the public would benefit from reduced energy prices and returns on public subsidies, and AI companies would avoid being blamed for high energy prices and poor grid reliability.

Bill Billman, Department of State, expressed concern that unprecedented, large-scale infrastructure projects are being proposed to meet what is a highly uncertain and ambiguous forecast of AI profitability. He also noted that the demand is relatively small compared to other energy demands, suggesting a need to take a step back and reflect on how complex and urgent the problem truly is. Benforado appreciated this perspective and said that the uncertainty makes it extremely challenging for grid and utility operators to plan and prepare. In his view, AI can improve the grid, accelerate decarbonization, and create revenue in the communities that host data centers. However, he said that those communities should maintain authority over these decisions, ensure public concerns are fully addressed, and investigate data centers' cumulative impacts, especially where they are clustered. Chien pointed out that while generative AI and ChatGPT are recent developments that have garnered a lot of attention, a broader suite of other AI technologies have become pervasive in many applications and have been successful for nearly a decade. Some projections may overstate future growth, but he said there is ample reason to believe that AI demand is not simply going to fizzle out.

Spurring Grid Modernization

Shenoy asked panelists to elaborate on opportunities for AI data centers to contribute to the overall modernization of the grid, in light of broader electrification trends. Sanders reiterated her view that the current attention on AI and data centers brings a powerful opportunity to drive progress in grid improvements more broadly and outlined several examples of policy ideas in this space. First, she said that policies are needed to encourage better leveraging of grid-enhancing innovations that enable capabilities such as increased situational awareness, efficiency standards for transmission lines, or reconductoring via advanced materials. Second, she said that the deployment of stable and dispatchable clean energy resources, nuclear power, and enhanced geothermal technologies can be accelerated with innovative financing structures such as clean tariffs, direct policies, or buyer's consortia. Third, intelligent demand-side management will require improved data sharing, privacy protections, and cybersecurity standards. Finally, she suggested fast-tracking creative interconnection and permitting plans that increase grid capacity, such as siting transmission lines along the federal highway system, employing AI to accelerate environmental permitting, and repurposing retired or underutilized connections.

All of these suggestions, Sanders continued, require regulations, structural reforms, and multi-stakeholder conversations to better align utilities' business models to reward responsible decarbonization strategies that also maximize community benefits. In addition, she emphasized the need for data center owners to become active partners in improving grid storage and resilience to extreme events. Herz pointed out that nuclear power will not progress until there is a safe system for controlling and disposing of waste.

7

Data Center Infrastructure

The design and operations of data centers have evolved over time and will need to continue to adapt in order to meet the rising energy demands of artificial intelligence (AI) workloads and achieve greater flexibility in their power consumption. To examine these data center infrastructure design and operation issues, Ayse Coskun, Boston University, moderated a session focused on coupling flexible computing and infrastructure management, including cooling, with realistic performance and sustainability goals, ensuring scalability and responsiveness in the face of AI-driven demand. The panelists were Peter de Bock, Department of Energy (DOE); Ricardo Bianchini, Microsoft Azure; Adam Wierman, California Institute of Technology and Verrus; and Andrew Chien, University of Chicago.

PANELIST REMARKS

Advancing Efficient Cooling Systems

Running the AI chips to support society's seemingly insatiable demand for AI applications requires a great deal of energy, and de Bock highlighted that a large portion of that energy demand comes from technologies used to keep information technology (IT) equipment cool. As the energy density of each server rack increases, this challenge only grows more acute. As a result, DOE has identified cooling technologies as an area ripe for efficiencies and innovations to alleviate the load on the grid and impacts on communities. de Bock described DOE's Advanced

Research Projects Agency–Energy Cooling Operations Optimized for Leaps in Energy, Reliability, and Carbon Hyperefficiency for Information Processing Systems (COOLERCHIPS) initiative, which aims to develop high-performance cooling systems for energy-efficient data centers to support a clean energy future.[1] Fifteen teams across industry and academia are working to reduce cooling energy needs by approximately 90 percent by designing innovative, reliable cooling systems that reduce strains on the grid and conserve limited resources such as energy and water, allowing more efficient use of grid connections. Ten of the awards are focusing on secondary cooling loop technologies; three are focusing on modular data center designs; one is advancing cooling, energy, and reliability tools; and one is focused on facilities and standards.

Evolving Data Center Energy Challenges in the Artificial Intelligence Era

Bianchini discussed how different AI processes influence the evolving energy demands of data centers. As other speakers noted, data center electricity demand is rapidly growing, potentially tripling—or more—by 2030.[2] While efficiency efforts and innovations such as virtualization, cloud computing, and greater power usage effectiveness (PUE) successfully reduced energy demand in the past, Bianchini said that new advances are needed in the AI era.

The two main workloads associated with AI, training and inference, have different power needs. Training is performed in batches with high spikes in power use to support massive synchronous computation, a pattern that causes enormous power swings that can destabilize the grid (Figure 7-1). Bianchini added that training error corrections, the treatment of hardware failures during training, a necessary step in building large language models (LLMs), adds to the energy-intensiveness of training by requiring repeatedly rolling the execution back and resuming from the last checkpoint.

By contrast, inference consumes much less power because it is an interactive computation with lower utilization. However, its two phases, the prompt phase and the token phase,[3] behave very differently, creating a challenge to optimize for these different behaviors. Another challenge is maximizing power oversubscription while retaining high inference performance.

---

[1] Advanced Research Projects Agency-Energy, n.d., "COOLERCHIPS," https://arpa-e.energy.gov/technologies/programs/coolerchips, accessed April 21, 2025.

[2] D. Patel, D. Nishball, and J. Eliahou Ontiveros, 2024, "AI Datacenter Energy Dilemma—Race for AI Datacenter Space," *Semi Analysis,* March 13, https://semianalysis.com/2024/03/13/ai-datacenter-energy-dilemma-race.

[3] The *prompt phase* is when a model processes input, while the token phase is when the model draws on memory to generate a response.

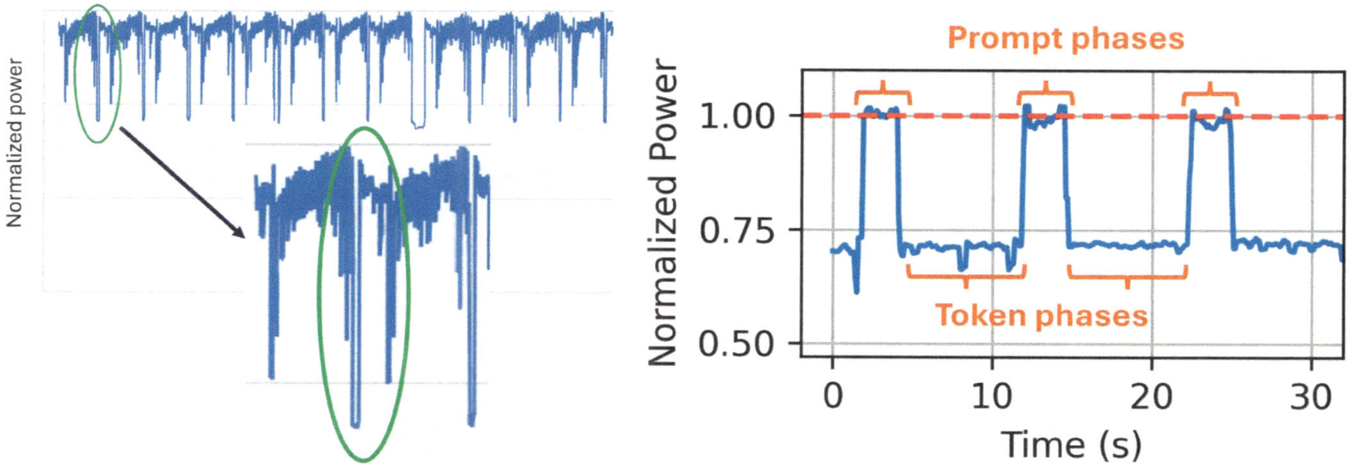

FIGURE 7-1 Artificial intelligence model power needs during training (*left*) and inference (*right*). These processes require different amounts of power and behave differently. Training involves wide swings in power usage that challenge utilities.
SOURCE: Ricardo Bianchini, Microsoft Azure, presentation to the workshop, November 12, 2024.

Toward a Dynamic and Cooperative Relationship Between Data Centers and the Grid

Chien highlighted recent trends in AI data center energy consumption and discussed opportunities to increase grid capacity and efficiency through more dynamic and cooperative relationships between data centers and the grid. The scale of computing power has grown by 50-fold over the decades, and the associated energy demand has also continued to skyrocket despite what Chien called "radical" improvements in energy efficiency for IT infrastructure.[4] The consequences of the current scale of data center operations, he said, include energy swings that destabilize the grid and power demands that far exceed its capabilities, neither of which can be addressed by energy efficiencies alone.

"I'm not going to dispute that energy efficiency is important, but it's not going to save us," Chien stated. Instead, he posited that new grid infrastructure and modernizations are needed to keep up with this growing demand, and that more capacity is needed, especially for renewable energy. In addition, he emphasized the importance of flexibility in data center energy needs in order to balance loads with the variable nature of renewable energy, which is increasingly being integrated into a grid that lacks storage or load management strategies to optimally handle variable renewable generation.[5] Echoing comments made by other speakers, Chien highlighted how data centers can act as a test case for grid modernization to support broader electrification trends. If their loads can be made dynamic and flexible, it is possible to support expanded grid capacity and increased efficiency while reducing costs, even as AI data centers continue to expand.[6] "Data centers, we believe, are actually—as the first leg of this electrification—the first model case for how you deal with these large adaptive loads effectively for the grid," Chien said. "And it turns out that if you can make your large, adaptive loads flexible, you can actually give a lot of benefits for the grid."

Making data centers more flexible is challenging, however, because they are cost-optimized capital investments that have to meet service-level objectives. Emerging ideas to increase efficiency include optimized scheduling, hyperscaling, and power management strategies. Looking forward,

[4] Goldman Sachs, 2024, "AI Is Poised to Drive 160% Increase in Data Center Power Demand," May 14, https://www.goldmansachs.com/insights/articles/AI-poised-to-drive-160-increase-in-power-demand.

[5] Energy Information Administration, 2025, "Short-Term Energy Outlook," https://www.eia.gov/outlooks/steo.

[6] L. Lin, R. Wijayawardana, V. Rao, H. Nguyen, E.W. Gnibga, and A.A. Chien, 2024, "Exploding AI Power Use: An Opportunity to Rethink Grid Planning and Management," Pp. 434–441 in *The 15th ACM International Conference on Future and Sustainable Energy Systems*, e-Energy '24, https://doi.org/10.1145/3632775.3661959.

Chien stressed the need for solutions to prevent data centers from becoming a "thundering herd" that crashes the grid or stresses its capacity to deliver clean energy. He added that fairness is also important, recognizing that large and small customers share the same grid and should bear the costs and benefits equally. To achieve this, he suggested that it may be necessary to incentivize flexibility through controlling load size or shape or encouraging consumption commitments to minimize the strain on the grid.

Designing Metrics to Drive Progress

Highlighting the role of metrics in driving progress, Wierman posited that new metrics are needed to support energy efficiency as AI data centers expand. The creation of PUE as a metric drove data centers' dramatic efficiency improvements in the past, and while PUE is fairly simple to measure and validate, it can be manipulated.[7] Two alternative metrics that have been proposed include carbon usage effectiveness (CUE), the ratio of carbon emissions to IT energy usage, and water usage effectiveness (WUE), the ratio of water usage to IT energy usage.

CUE and WUE have not yet been widely adopted, but Wierman said that they have already proven useful in identifying inefficiencies and driving improvements in data center infrastructure designs. However, they do not capture everything; for example, other metrics may be needed to address factors such as workload patterns, synchronicity, flexibility, grid integration, operational versus embedded carbon, and the role of power purchase agreements versus onsite renewable generation.

Many communities have expressed resistance to hosting data centers; Wierman noted that concerns about noise, utility impacts, and increased emissions and pollution can complicate siting and construction and constrain AI growth.[8,9,10,11] Perhaps even more important are the signifi-

---

[7] R. Bianchini, C. Belady, and A. Sivasubramaniam, 2024, "Data Center Power and Energy Management: Past, Present, and Future," *IEEE Micro* 44(5):30–36, https://doi.org/10.1109/MM.2024.3426478.

[8] P. Pineda, 2021, "Unsustainable, Resource-Hungry and Loud: Why Chandler Wants to Ban More Data Centers," *AZ Central,* November 22, https://www.azcentral.com/story/news/local/chandler/2021/11/22/chandler-wants-ban-more-data-centers-after-years-complaints/8627569002.

[9] D. Geiger and E. Thomas, 2024, "Electric Grids Need Upgrades Thanks to Data Centers. Guess Who Helps Pay for That," *Business Insider,* April 18, https://www.businessinsider.com/data-centers-electricity-consumers-discounts-utilities-2024-4.

[10] C. O'Donovan, 2024, "Fighting Back Against Data Centers, One Small Town at a Time," *Washington Post,* October 5, https://www.washingtonpost.com/technology/2024/10/05/data-center-protest-community-resistance.

[11] E. Halper, 2024, "A Utility Promised to Stop Burning Coal. Then Google and Meta Came to Town," *Washington Post,* October 12, https://www.washingtonpost.com/business/2024/10/08/google-meta-omaha-data-centers.

cant health impacts data centers can inflict on communities. Even with the lower-end estimates of data center growth, the health costs related to data center emissions for the United States as a whole are projected to exceed on-road emissions in the state of California by 2030. The health costs associated with these emissions rival data centers' electricity costs and are particularly high in low-income communities. In light of these important concerns and impacts of data center expansion, Wierman challenged attendees to consider what metrics might be most useful in driving progress toward cleaner and more just practices in the future.

PANEL DISCUSSION

Participants discussed a wide range of opportunities for evaluating and optimizing data center infrastructure to address impacts on the grid, local communities, and the environment.

Opportunities for Optimizing Data Centers

Coskun asked the panelists to name what they see as the most important changes to data center design and operation that are needed to meet the growing AI demand. Underscoring the need for a more holistic approach to data center design, de Bock suggested viewing data centers as essentially one large computer whose every element, from a chip to the entire building, must be fully optimized for energy efficiency. Current metrics fail to capture this full spectrum, and even the term "data center" lacks a clear definition, but he suggested that lessons could be gleaned from other fields—such as aerospace reliability metrics—to inform new and more holistic approaches. He added that there could also be opportunities to redesign AI algorithms with increased reliability to improve efficiency and minimize failures and energy-intensive resets. Bianchini agreed but noted that optimizing every layer of a data center poses an enormous challenge. For instance, he noted that cooling systems will need to change from air cooling to liquid cooling methods (e.g., cold plates for direct-to-chip cooling), power-delivery systems will need to change as rack power densities grow exponentially, the power swings of large-scale training need to be mitigated, and AI models themselves need efficiency improvements. Every layer presents unique problems—and opportunities—for innovation.

Wierman added that the uncertainty and rapid growth in AI makes these tasks even more daunting and highlighted the value of building more flexibility into every design element. Chien agreed that new metrics should be designed to incentivize flexibility and sustainability, adding that solutions need to be cost-effective to ensure wide implementation.

Interacting with the grid today is not cost-effective, and while that is an enormous challenge, there are solutions. For example, data centers that have flexible loads and span multiple municipalities can more easily harmonize with multiple grids and leverage demand response programs.

Bianchini added that certain grid interactions require active "load shedding," and optimizing data centers against this is another large challenge. Wierman said that cost-effective, flexibility-supporting infrastructure improvements, such as onsite electricity storage, can help to address this. Like de Bock, he pointed to aerospace for models and suggested using service-level agreements that specify reliability levels for particular situations. It may also be possible to create a new metric that quantifies a data center's flexibility to enable better comparisons and inform decision-making.

Given the large and growing number of chips in AI data centers, de Bock highlighted the importance of incorporating flexibility in cooling. In addition, he noted that it is difficult to ensure reliability when it is unclear if the grid can deliver the power needed. Data center owners may find it more cost-effective to build and control their own smaller power plants, which puts pressure on the grid and makes integration challenging but also has benefits, as having highly reliable power will enhance flexibility for meeting data centers' dynamic loads. Building on this point, Bianchini noted that grid stability is just as important as cost-effectiveness, if not more so, especially as the grid integrates more renewable energy sources and attempts to handle more power swings. Data center siting can impact this stability, and de Bock described the current situation as akin to a "tightrope walker" balancing supply and demand on a grid that was not built for today's needs.

Accounting for Data Center Impacts

Panelists discussed approaches for including various types of impacts of data centers in thinking about optimizing data center infrastructure moving forward. Laura Gonzalez Guerrero, Clean Virginia, asked about appropriate methods for accounting for externalities such as health impacts. As the technology industry races ahead to expand data center infrastructure, Bianchini said that it is important for utilities and governments to agree on how such externalities are measured and paid for. Chien expressed his view that utilities could likely price data centers' energy costs differently without slowing down growth, as companies are already agreeing to pay above-market prices to ensure energy supply. Wierman agreed and noted that extra energy costs are considered nominal because the most important resources that data center owners consider are access to land and access to energy. Coskun noted that more research is needed to better understand how the cost of operational electricity factors into data centers' costs.

Coskun prompted panelists to elaborate on proposed metrics for efficiency, sustainability, and health care costs. Wierman replied that the health care cost metrics his group used were created through established models, such as models developed by the U.S. Environmental Protection Agency, for example, linking cases of asthma to extra emissions, in order to better reflect how data centers impact communities and grids. He added that developing better metrics in this area would also improve siting and design negotiations between utilities and data center developers. Bianchini agreed with Wierman's point that PUE is flawed and changes or new metrics are needed. However, he said that there is no consensus on potential solutions nor is there quality data to enact them. "We're nowhere near having a good set of metrics," he stated.

Chien agreed that better metrics are needed and added that advancing sustainability goals through carbon accounting poses another challenge, but this is a challenge that needs to be addressed across all of society, not by industry alone. He suggested a more direct attribution of emissions to their sources could help to incentivize behavior change. Another challenge has been how flexibility impacts different grid settings. On this issue, he said that two potential solutions are adding more capacity or changing generation load duties. Unfortunately, adaptive loads can impact computing and may require another metric to capture and alter it, but he expressed confidence that flexibility solutions are coming.

While he said that the focus on PUE has been instrumental in creating improvements, de Bock also agreed that new metrics are needed, especially to compare the many new cooling technologies. To this end, he said that the COOLERCHIPS initiative is creating better definitions of PUE denominator and rack density, and adding local weather inputs to test models in challenging climates. Metrics of consideration include total power usage effectiveness and IT power usage effectiveness. However, there is very little public reporting of water and electricity use, making it challenging to get a full picture of the growth that is happening and its possible impacts.

Interactions with the Grid

Data centers do not only cause negative impacts, de Bock noted; they also create tax revenue and other benefits for communities. Under new policies, they could also generate and share their own power through microgrids that add capacity to the larger grid. Bianchini noted that large cloud providers are already exploring the idea of microgrids in some cases. A participant asked if data centers could become "first-class" actors on the grid, meaning they have some control and scheduling power over their load even during power swings, enhancing grid stability. Chien replied that the distinction between data centers as independent actors and as first-class actors speaks to the heart of the problem. Grid operations are designed to control electric power service while maintaining stability and resilience for the whole grid, rather than to provide resilience for any particular load. Since data centers are not primarily run for the benefit of the grid, having more control in the hands of these entities would not necessarily align with grid operators' objectives, and resistance to data sharing and transparency on the part of data centers could make it difficult to accomplish this level of cooperation anyway.

Building on the points panelists made about the need for metrics that are relevant to key goals, Line Roald, University of Wisconsin–Madison, proposed using cost-usage effectiveness to capture the price that data centers pay in electricity markets. This metric can help data centers prioritize their workloads by reacting to price signals, which improves grid stability and communities' understanding of their impacts, she said. Wierman expressed support for Roald's suggestion and agreed that measuring data center–grid interactions could shed light on the services data centers provide and the cost impacts of data center flexibilities. He noted that some European grids are experimenting with prioritizing interconnections depending on what a given data center is doing, and while enforcement could be challenging, it is important to consider new ideas as data centers create power constraints that affect activities across society. However, Chien said he is not sure such an approach would be in line with the United States' open-market principles that allow different valuations of an activity amid different resource allocation. Certainly, critical infrastructure such as hospitals must be prioritized, but he said that in commerce, it is very hard to harmonize resource prioritization and allocation, especially globally.

Data Center Siting

Eric Masanet, University of California, Santa Barbara, asked what factors influence the siting of large training data centers. Bianchini replied that a cool climate, plentiful water, sufficient grid capacity, and a lack of competition over resources are needed. However, he cautioned that training should not be the focus, because the training infrastructure will be substantially smaller than the inference infrastructure and will not be easily monetized. Given the interactivity and latency constraints of inference, Bianchini and de Bock noted that the data centers to support this aspect of AI are unlikely to be located very far from the customer base. The siting priorities for data centers have changed over time, de Bock added, evolving from a focus on where the best networks were, to where land was cheap, to where power is available. He also added that cooling is a solvable problem that will expand siting flexibility and enable data centers to operate in warmer climates, which is important because warmer places also tend to have more wind and solar power, which keeps energy prices low. He speculated that different types of data center designs may develop in response to differing operations, energy needs, and latency constraints.

Chien noted that inference and training are dynamic activities with different latency requirements. Today's users are tolerating longer latencies, and combining that with emerging inference workloads creates more flexibility for data center locations.

Capturing Artificial Intelligence Costs and Benefits

A participant asked how metrics can reflect the trade-offs involved in AI's impacts on the economy and society, both locally and globally. Chien suggested it may be too early to place a value on AI's positive impacts because it can take years before adoption is widespread enough to see productivity gains. Bianchini agreed that adoption can take decades—AI is advancing much faster than other technologies, and while many benefits can be envisioned, it will be a long time before AI tools are fully established in daily life. In his view, de Bock stated that one of AI's most valuable contributions to date is natural language processing. While this capability enables people to more effectively interact with computers without specialized expertise, he acknowledged that the exact benefit of this is hard to measure. As to drawbacks, de Bock noted that many data centers use noisy, diesel-powered generators as backup power sources, highlighting the need for new technologies such as innovative battery designs. Wierman agreed that AI improvements also come with costs, and it is important to be able to measure and balance both the benefits and the costs.

Advancing Flexibility

One participant asked panelists to comment on why flexibility is seen as so important when the future of AI is inference, which is latency sensitive and not especially flexible. Wierman replied that apart from workloads, there are many infrastructure opportunities for improving flexibility, such as oversubscription and onsite energy storage, which are becoming increasingly cost-effective as they scale up. Chien added that rather than turn workloads on or off, there are flexibility opportunities within the applications themselves, such as using smaller models or constraining computation when power prices rise. In addition, de Bock suggested the potential for modularized data centers that are dynamically located and equipped according to an expanding reference design to address these issues, but he noted that they would need new fiber optic networks to offset energy or latency needs.

Additional Environmental Considerations

Erma Leaphart-Gooch, Sierra Club Michigan, asked panelists to comment on data centers' impacts on source water and the potential to use geothermal energy to supplement other energy sources. While geothermal energy is low carbon and has large-scale potential, de Bock said that there are many steps before it will be ready for broader deployment in the United States. As for water, de Bock noted that some current data centers use water in outside evaporative cooling towers, but the COOLERCHIPS initiative could help to identify more sustainable innovations that would eliminate the need for water evaporation. Wierman agreed that data centers' water use is an important issue, and said that its impacts on the local environment and public health should be explicitly measured. Bianichini also agreed and noted that many hyperscale companies are moving away from evaporation towers.

8

Efficiency Through Technology Advancement: Hardware–Software Interactions

In a keynote presentation and panel discussion, participants examined opportunities to improve carbon efficiency and sustainability through the coordinated design of hardware and software. William Dally, NVIDIA, set the stage for the discussion with a keynote presentation describing the major contributors to the large energy efficiency gains seen in both hardware and software for large language models (LLMs) over the past decade and what the future may hold for further developments in hardware and model efficiency. Panelists then delivered opening remarks outlining the landscape of hardware platforms and the role of specialized architectures for artificial intelligence (AI), and Dally and other panelists explored the software strategies required to achieve high performance and efficiency on these architectures in an open discussion.

KEYNOTE PRESENTATION

Dally highlighted how AI developments have accelerated energy demands and described some of the factors that may influence this trajectory in the future.[1] While huge efficiency gains have been achieved—today's AI chips are upward of 1,000 times more efficient than their predecessors—some experts subscribe to Jevons paradox, that more efficiency will just create more demand. To meet this demand, companies will

[1] K. Bourzac, 2024, "Fixing AI's Energy Crisis," *Nature*, October 17, https://doi.org/10.1038/d41586-024-03408-z.

seek to build AI data centers wherever power generation can be quickly ramped up. Because this is generally a slower process in the United States than some other countries, Dally posited that challenges with energy capacity not only represent an important issue for the U.S. grid but pose a threat to the United States' dominance in AI.

Dally offered context on why AI data centers have such large energy demands. A primary driver is the energy required for model training. The amount of floating-point operations per second required to train models has gone up by a factor of 10^7 and is still increasing by more than an order of magnitude each year. In addition, inference is representing a growing share of AI activities, albeit more slowly. Every AI model is also conducting more operations per second, and more models are being deployed across more applications, such as medicine, science, and entertainment, creating more potential value and further driving demand.[2] Finally, AI models are becoming more complicated, with more steps requiring more energy.

AI demand is not going away, but Dally posited that its energy needs can be minimized through continual hardware and software innovations and optimizations. He highlighted how the significant gains made in AI chips' energy efficiency and performance over the past decade (Figure 8-1) did not come from smaller transistors and process technology improvements, but from improving number representation. Using fewer bits to represent numbers (going from 32 to just 4) has made instructions more efficient. As a result, extra processing overhead has dropped to less than 10 percent. In addition, structured sparsity schemes make algorithms much more efficient while preserving accuracy, although more research is needed to build effective sparse matrix graphics processing unit (GPU) hardware.[3,4] NVIDIA's current GPU has 20 PetaFLOPS available for inference operations, providing state-of-the-art efficiency and performance. Higher-density racks also improve efficiency, because communication at close range takes less energy. Next-generation technology will provide 100 TeraOPS/W for even more efficiency.[5] Software efficiency has also

[2] E. Masanet, A. Shehabi, N. Lei, S. Smith, and J. Koomey, 2020, "Recalibrating Global Data Center Energy-Use Estimates," *Science* 367(6481):984–986, https://doi.org/10.1126/science.aba3758.

[3] NVIDIA, n.d., *NVIDIA A100 Tensor Core GPU Architecture: Unprecedented Acceleration at Every Scale,* https://images.nvidia.com/aem-dam/en-zz/Solutions/data-center/nvidia-ampere-architecture-whitepaper.pdf, accessed December 15, 2024.

[4] A. Mishra, J.A. Latorre, J. Pool, et al., 2021, "Accelerating Sparse Deep Neural Networks," arXiv:2104.08378, https://doi.org/10.48550/arXiv.2104.08378.

[5] B. Keller, R. Venkatesan, S. Dai, S.G. Tell, B. Zimmer, and W.J. Dally, 2022, "A 17–95.6 TOPS/W Deep Learning Inference Accelerator with Per-Vector Scaled 4-Bit Quantization for Transformers in 5nm," Pp. 16–17 in *2022 IEEE Symposium on VLSI Technology and Circuits (VLSI Technology and Circuits),* https://doi.org/10.1109/VLSITechnologyandCir46769.2022.9830277.

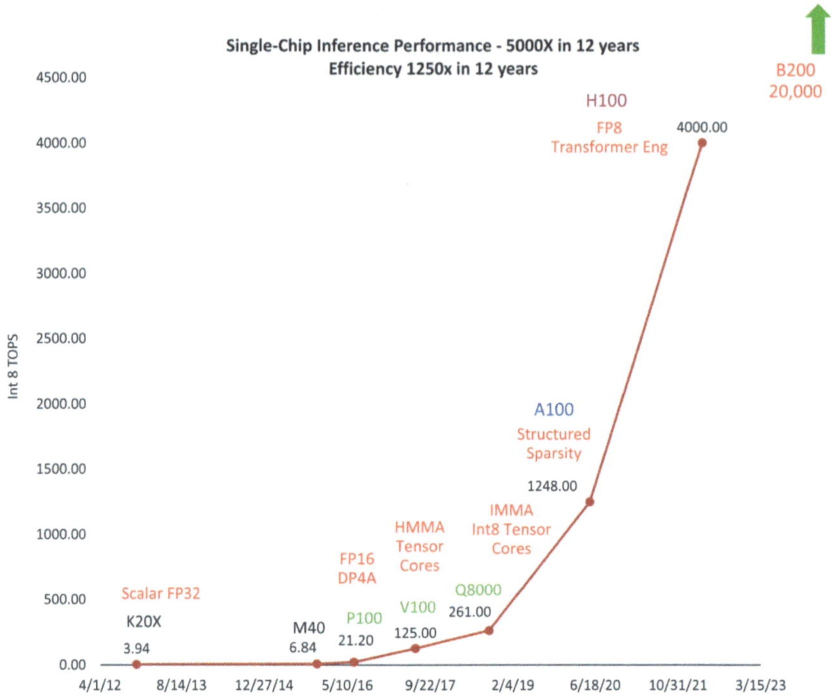

FIGURE 8-1 Trends in artificial intelligence chip performance, 2012–2023.
SOURCE: William Dally, NVIDIA, presentation to the workshop, November 13, 2024.

improved. Structured sparsity also improves neural networks through pruning and retraining.[6] As a result of all of these developments, between 2012 and 2024, it is estimated that single-chip inference performance increased by 5,000-fold, AI hardware efficiency increased by 1,250-fold, and AI software efficiency increased by more than 1,000-fold, Dally said.

Looking forward, Dally outlined several drivers that can continue this trajectory toward even greater efficiency. First, he suggested focusing on efficiency alongside accuracy as a standard evaluation metric for AI innovations. Second, researchers are exploring how efficiency might be improved by implementing state–space models in place of transformer architectures, which are expensive in comparison, or hybrids of

[6] R. Venkatesan, Y.S. Shao, M. Wang, J. Clemons, S. Dai, and M. Fojtik, 2019, "MAGNet: A Modular Accelerator Generator for Neural Networks," Pp. 1–8 in *2019 IEEE/ACM International Conference on Computer-Aided Design (ICCAD)*, https://doi.org/10.1109/ICCAD45719.2019.8942127.

the two approaches. Finally, he suggested efficiency gains could be made by implementing smaller, more specialized models through distillation, retraining, and fine-tuning.[7]

Discussion

In a question-and-answer session, participants delved deeper into AI efficiency and then discussed several considerations at the intersection of data centers and the electric power grid. Andrew Chien, University of Chicago, asked how NVIDIA was making GPUs efficient during the AI training phase, especially as size and capacity increases. Dally replied that it is harder to measure training efficiency than inference efficiency, and therefore harder to reduce the precision on training, but NVIDIA's chips have no loss of accuracy for inference. Moving from single GPUs to clusters also increases efficiency if the units are located close together, making high-bandwidth communication cheaper and more efficient. Communication efficiency innovations also mean that most of the energy demand is from computation. As racks get larger, they do use more power, but it is still relatively inexpensive and efficient at scale and compared to alternatives.

A participant asked Dally what other hardware innovations can improve energy efficiency. He replied that there is potential in increasing sparsity on weights and activations, and also in number representation. He added that very aggressive packaging could also reduce the communication and data movement energy needed. Improvements are unlikely to come from smaller transistors or more advanced process nodes, however. Another participant asked if there are trade-offs between increased efficiency and security. Dally replied that there are not, stating that NVIDIA's chips are fully secure, with efficiencies safely located within GPUs' secure enclaves.

Carole-Jean Wu, Meta, asked about energy efficiencies related to cooling requirements. Dally said he did not have the data on this and does not know if the energy required to chill water is accounted for, but believes the energy required to actually pump chilled water through the racks is not a substantial portion of the total energy used to run the AI systems.

Participants then turned to the interactions between AI data centers and the grid. Tamar Eilam, IBM Research, asked how AI workloads can support flexibility within the power grid. Dally replied that the level of fine-grain control over GPUs should mean that there is no technical challenge with this, but there may be an economic one, as companies

---

[7] S.T. Sreenivas, S. Muralidharan, R. Joshi, et al., 2024, "LLM Pruning and Distillation in Practice: The Minitron Approach," arXiv:2408.11796, https://doi.org/10.48550/arXiv.2408.11796.

that buy expensive equipment may be reluctant to reduce performance when, for example, there is not enough renewable energy available to run them.

Another participant asked where Dally would expect new, large-scale data centers to be built, if not in the United States. He replied that it may be possible that parts of Texas and the western United States could be areas for growth in this space, but in general he speculated that countries with sufficient wealth, fewer regulatory hurdles, or both—such as in the Middle East or South America—are the most likely to attract data centers.

Asked about AI data centers' storage and networking requirements, Dally noted that networking needs increase quite a bit, especially with large training clusters. They also go up during inference as external clients connect. Storage is less clear, because while data centers have to store all of the weights that the different models serve, it may plateau as the number of models and weights stabilizes. Another participant asked if interconnection speeds will also increase. Dally replied that they had been rapidly increasing but are at a plateau now until fundamental blockers can be removed. One potential solution is optical GPU interconnection, which offers increased efficiency and performance and is already implemented in long-distance interconnects.

Wu asked if fault tolerance or failures pose concerns with large-scale computing arrays. Dally replied that they are concerning because they can require disruptive restarts. Switching from checkpoint restarts to continual computations helps, as does replacing the faulting or failing piece. That switch will disrupt the bulk synchronous nature of AI training, however, and so NVIDIA is searching for a solution that balances the load more equitably without slowing computation.

PANELIST REMARKS

Wu moderated a panel discussion focused on opportunities to make efficiency gains through technological advancements in hardware–software interactions to balance AI's exponential growth. The panelists were Miloš Popovic, Ayar Labs; Eilam; Valerie Taylor, Argonne National Laboratory; Vivienne Sze, Massachusetts Institute of Technology; and Dally.

Improving Artificial Intelligence Infrastructure Efficiency with Optical Input-Output

AI processors have made great gains in density, but these architectures are currently limited by data bandwidth and data movement. Popovic described how optical interconnection (also known as optical input-output or optical I/O[8]) will soon be able to solve both of these problems and substantially improve the efficiency of AI hardware.

Light traveling through optical fiber minimizes bandwidth needs because it takes less space than an electrical signal through a wire, and many wavelengths fit on the same fiber. As a result, more data—orders of magnitude more—can be passed through a single strand.[9] In addition, optical interconnection provides distance-independent energy consumption, as opposed to wires, whose energy use is proportional to distance. Finally, optics need very little energy to move data when they are close to and deeply integrated with computing elements.

Current processors that use optical interconnection have both efficiencies and limitations.[10] To make progress, Ayar Labs scientists have experimented with optically interconnected GPUs and divided workloads and found a 20-fold improvement in energy efficiency, especially when implementing parallel programming across multiple processors. This demonstrates how optical I/O could enable future growth in the number of interconnected GPUs with minimal limitations.

Innovating for Efficiency Across the Artificial Intelligence Stack

Despite the many efficiencies implemented thus far, Eilam said that additional innovations across every layer of the AI stack are needed to minimize energy demands. For example, she said that fit-for-purpose, domain-specific accelerators; new tools or architectures to break the Von Neumann memory bottleneck; and packaging efficiencies are needed. She added that new model architectures, perhaps based on the mechanics of the human brain, which is irregular and domain-specific, could also enhance efficiency.

Model innovation is also needed to create smaller AI models that are carefully trained and fine-tuned, use sequence or state space, and can be reused or used in collaboration. The AI platform itself is the glue holding models and systems together, and she suggested that AI platforms could be made more efficient by better integrating heterogeneous accelerators to raise the level of abstraction; better matching models and accelerators; building in observability, transparency, trust, and community; and optimizing and scaling workloads.

---

[8] Optical I/O uses light instead of electrical signals to transfer data.

[9] D.A.B. Miller, 1990, "A New Principle of Wave Propagation: Huygens' Principle Corrected After 300 Years," in *Optical Society of America Annual Meeting,* Technical Digest Series, PDP16, https://doi.org/10.1364/OAM.1990.PDP16.

[10] M. Wade, E. Anderson, S. Ardalan, et al., 2021, "An Error-Free 1 Tbps WDM Optical I/O Chiplet and Multi-Wavelength Multi-Port Laser," in *Optical Fiber Communication Conference (OFC),* OSA Technical Digest F3C.6, Optica Publishing Group, https://doi.org/10.1364/OFC.2021.F3C.6.

IBM researchers are working on these issues. One prototype accelerator, with fit-for-purpose integrated design and specific values and requirements, supports specializations such as fraud detection and geospatial analysis. A second, with an innovative, brain-inspired approach to memory, is extremely energy efficient but can currently only support smaller models.

Near- and Long-Term Impacts of Hardware–Software Co-Design

Taylor described opportunities to reduce AI data center energy demands through effective hardware–software co-design. A long-term vision for co-design includes synergy across the entire AI design stack, from materials and physics to devices, integration, architectures, algorithms, and applications.[11] While this process has been employed for adjacent AI layers, Taylor emphasized that an all-to-all and holistic co-design approach—including materials researchers, applications experts, and everyone in between collaborating on power, speed, and space—would have a large impact.

One co-design project, Threadwork, is a collaboration between Argonne, Northwestern University, and the University of Chicago that investigates optical interconnection applications in high-energy physics and neuromorphic materials and has developed devices with significantly reduced power needs.[12]

Hardware–software co-design can also have near-term impacts on efficiency. Hardware trends include innovating memory access to reduce data movement, using mixed- and low-precision computations, and considering biologically inspired hardware.[13] Software trends, such as LLM inference benchmarks, explore different open source LLMs, AI accelerators, and inference frameworks for improved efficiency.[14]

[11] C. Murray, S. Guha, D. Reed, et al., 2018, *Basic Research Needs for Microelectronics: Report of the Office of Science Workshop on Basic Research Needs for Microelectronics October 23–25, 2018,* Technical Report, Department of Energy, Office of Science, https://doi.org/10.2172/1616249.

[12] Argonne National Laboratory, n.d., "Threadwork," https://www.anl.gov/threadwork, accessed April 21, 2025.

[13] N.P. Jouppi, D.H. Yoon, M. Ashcraft, M. Gottscho, T.B. Jablin, and G. Kurian, 2021, "Ten Lessons from Three Generations Shaped Google's TPUv4i: Industrial Product," Pp. 1–14 in *2021 ACM/IEEE 48th Annual International Symposium on Computer Architecture (ISCA),* https://doi.org/10.1109/ISCA52012.2021.00010.

[14] K.T. Chitty-Venkata, S. Raskar, B. Kale, et al., 2024, "LLM-Inference-Bench: Inference Benchmarking of Large Language Models on AI Accelerators," arXiv:2411.00136, https://doi.org/10.48550/arXiv.2411.00136.

Moving Data More Efficiently

Sze discussed opportunities to co-design AI hardware and software to improve the efficiency of data movement. Data movement dominates AI energy consumption, much more so than computing.[15] It is possible to reduce the *amount* of data movement through computing-in-memory strategies or data reuse, where data is moved once to be used in multiple operations. It is also possible to reduce the *energy* that the data movement requires, by bringing chips or chiplets closer together, using 3D stacking to minimize the distance the data must travel, or by implementing optical interconnection or superconductors. However, these methods face a variety of challenges including manufacturing costs, yield, robustness, cooling, and scaling.

Co-designing models and hardware could also reduce the energy per computation and the amount of computation by reducing the precision or numeric representation, reducing model sizes through specialization or new model architecture, and exploiting sparsity, Sze said. Accomplishing these energy savings will often require hardware support and reducing the energy of the model needs to be balanced with maintaining accuracy. Considering these workload demands from an applications perspective can also allow one to exploit redundancies, enabling another form of sparsity.

More specialized hardware can improve efficiency, but Sze noted that this may come with trade-offs with regard to flexibility. It is often not preferred to hard-code AI models into the hardware because they have very different weights and architectures. In addition, while the hardware can be specialized in many ways, from instructions to dataflow and mapping, it is challenging to balance that specialization with future-proofing and unexpected limitations to innovation.

A Decade of Efficiency Gains

Dally highlighted some of the history he shared in his keynote presentation regarding drivers of increasing efficiency in AI systems over the past decade. GPUs are increasingly energy efficient thanks to innovations in number representation, complex instructions, and sparsity. Dally commented that the first two methods are largely mined out and said that the next generation of efficiencies will come from better leveraging sparsity. In addition, he noted that large gains are possible from hardware and software improvements and specialized models with improved attention.

---

[15] M. Horowitz, 2014, "1.1 Computing's Energy Problem (and What We Can Do About It)," Pp. 10–14 in *2014 IEEE International Solid-State Circuits Conference Digest of Technical Papers (ISSCC)*, https://doi.org/10.1109/ISSCC.2014.6757323.

These innovations can help fuel the "AI gold rush" and enable society to fully leverage its benefits.

PANEL DISCUSSION

In an open discussion, panelists examined opportunities for hardware efficiencies and their adoption timelines, considerations around operational versus embodied carbon, data center needs, and future directions.

Hardware Efficiencies and Adoption Timelines

Wu asked how long it would take to start seeing efficiency gains from the technological solutions the panelists identified during their opening remarks. Dally replied that it depends on the length of testing and software adaptation, but generally it takes 1–2 years for a new GPU to make an impact. Popovic noted that optical interconnection has been possible for more than a decade, but it was not used or useful until it gained high-volume capabilities, and its manufacturing ecosystem still needs 2–3 years to develop for it to have a large-scale impact. Dally agreed, noting that many new technologies start this way—several breakthroughs are needed before an innovation reaches a stage where it can be easily built; is energy efficient; and has an obvious use, a ready audience, and no viable alternatives.

Eilam noted that some of the solutions she named were more long term, radical, and potentially very rewarding and should be pursued despite the risks or trade-offs. In addition, hardware–software co-design will provide support for software efficiency gains and architecture improvements and could identify different neural network archetypes that are more suitable for different use cases and architecture designs. In the nearer term, she said that many solutions are already in use, such as reduced precision, alternative architectures, modular chiplets, and 3D stacking. Taylor agreed, adding that gains from co-designing with materials scientists has long-term potential to greatly impact energy use and emissions output.

Wu asked when software engineers can exploit the efficiency potential from hardware innovations. Dally replied that they can do so immediately, because AI systems are poised to quickly integrate modifications and new features. Eilam suggested that software engineers are also more amenable to AI adaptations because the timing is right—it has a potentially enormous payoff, and the limits of scaling laws have been reached.

Noting that AI is not yet profitable, Popovic said that hardware efficiencies are needed to enable developers to layer applications on top of AI models to make them more economically viable. If that does not happen, he speculated that efficiency gains will be moot. Dally argued that that scenario was unlikely in light of current momentum toward monetizing AI.

A participant asked if there were memory or virtualization innovations in the pipeline. Dally replied that the question of how much memory to add to GPUs depends on a complicated balance of cost, usefulness, capacity, and access, and this calculation is re-optimized with every new generation. NVIDIA is considering putting memory directly on top of a GPU, bringing it closer, and further reducing energy costs, but that will also limit capacity and could potentially bring issues with power distribution and thermal regulation. Virtualization is less of a problem, however, as having 100 percent virtual memory in one space increases bandwidth, Dally said.

Eilam noted that IBM took the opposite path—their chip has only static RAM with no external memory, a fit-for-purpose design that has proven successful with smaller models. Taylor added that some scientific applications require significant memory and are moving toward surrogate models that change the ratio of computing to memory. "Memristors," or memory resistors, could help navigate these different memory demands, she noted.

Ayse Coksun, Boston University, asked about power management. Dally agreed that there are opportunities to improve power management, many of which NVIDIA already uses. Their chips react quickly to power fluctuations by running at full speed, changing states to stay within a thermal envelope, and employing frequency-adaptive delay lock loops. NVIDIA researchers are also investigating more efficient power converters to react quickly to load variation. Taylor added that there are also opportunities across different AI accelerators, as each has its own power monitoring library with a distinct functionality, to create more uniformity of monitoring that could be reported to users.

A participant asked if it was possible to use AI to recode software in order to help free up data center capacity. Taylor replied that it is possible, noting that Argonne is working on using LLMs to translate its software, but researchers are encountering verification challenges, compiling errors, and, importantly, performance issues.

Reid Lifset, Yale University, asked about the potential for reuse of AI hardware. Dally replied that outdated hardware should be retired if the goal is to improve energy efficiency. While it could be resold, "it's better to move on to the latest technology because it's the most efficient," he stated. Dally also confirmed that Jevons paradox, where use increases as efficiency rises and costs fall, is already happening in AI. Eilam suggested that scientists or innovative technology cannot solve Jevons paradox—that is a matter for government and policy—but they can focus on reducing the energy demands of computation.

Operational Versus Embodied Carbon

While many of the innovations panelists described in their remarks are relevant to reducing the carbon generated through AI system operations, Wu asked panelists to comment on the balance of operational versus embodied carbon and what energy demands might be anticipated with manufacturing new hardware and accelerators. Dally suggested that operational carbon deserves more of the focus, as embodied carbon accounts for only a small portion of a GPU's life-cycle carbon impact. Sze countered that both areas need to be considered. For example, it is possible that more specialized hardware will have a shorter lifespan as it might not be able to support new models and thus require more frequent replacement. It is important to find the right balance.

Eilam added that it is important to look at life-cycle trade-offs when weighing embodied carbon—embedded redundancies have fewer errors and extended lifetimes but can increase manufacturing costs or emissions. For example, IBM's explorations into perfluoroalkyl substance replacements cannot be fully electrified, making it harder to reduce embodied emissions. Andrew Grimshaw, Lancium, noted that some vendors publish information about embodied and operational carbon in their product documentation.

Data Center Needs

Panelists then turned to considerations around data center siting and associated needs, drivers, and impacts. Grimshaw suggested that data centers should be located in places where renewable energy is cheap and power usage effectiveness (PUE) would be ideal, instead of clustering in places like Virginia. Dally noted that some developers already use this approach; for example, this is the reason why many cryptocurrency data centers were built in Washington State where they could use excess hydropower. "I think it's just a great concept to be putting the computer where the power is cheap, because it's easier to move the bits around than it is to move the watts around," he noted. In his view, however, he said that PUE is not a good measure of efficiency because it requires GPUs to run at high temperature, which increases leakage current and hence power dissipation. Instead, he suggested using the ratio of total power versus total computing as measured in OPS, not watts.

Laura Gonzalez Guerrero, Clean Virginia, asked what data centers can do today to avoid increasing fossil fuel use. Dally suggested moving data centers to west Texas where they can access cheap energy. Wu pointed out that there are other considerations, and a participant listed the cost of land and equipment, permitting ease, and latency concerns as key additional considerations, although given how fast signals travel today, latency is perhaps less of an issue. Eilam agreed that data center location requires careful consideration, especially with regard to renewable energy availability and grid reliability.

Future Directions

To close the session, Wu asked each panelist to identify an important area of research and investment. Eilam expressed excitement about the future—and current—value of AI and suggested it could greatly accelerate scientific discovery—for example, by solving hard problems in medicine and materials science. She identified a need for more investment in hardware–software co-design, especially algorithm innovation in neural network architecture. AI also has the potential to accelerate renewable energy production and use if computing can fully leverage its flexibility.

Taylor expressed agreement regarding the importance of co-design and reiterated the need for a holistic examination and optimization of the full AI stack, from materials to applications. Dally named two areas: exploiting sparsity of activations in hardware design and, in software, replacing transformers' reliance on quadratic complexity with a more efficient approach. Popovic highlighted the need for more investment in education. Sze echoed the importance of holistic co-design and suggested that different research communities, which are currently siloed, should work together to create a shared language for full system optimization. She also noted that it is important to understand how to use AI selectively, when the job or costs make it worthwhile.

A

Statement of Task

The National Academies of Sciences, Engineering, and Medicine will organize a public workshop to explore trends, drivers, and implications of data center electricity use and greenhouse gas emissions related to artificial intelligence. The workshop will bring together a diverse group of expert stakeholders from the electricity industry, the computing industry including producers and users of artificial intelligence (AI), and the policy-making and regulatory community to discuss areas such as:

- Trends, drivers, and trade-offs related to AI that have the potential to impact energy demands;
- Application of AI tools to facilitate energy and water efficiency improvements in data centers;
- Standardizing benchmarks and accounting methods for energy efficiency and carbon emissions within the Information Technology sector;
- Trends in electricity markets, electrification, and options for all sectors to meet net-zero goals under increased demand for electricity;
- Regional considerations related to data center siting and clean generation resource availability.

The aim of the workshop is to understand how to map, measure, and mitigate the impacts of AI as they relate to data center electricity usage. Possible outcomes include describing the proportion of current data center electricity use and emissions related to AI; identifying a range of scenarios for potential increased electricity use and emissions; identifying options to mitigate potential increased electricity use and emissions; and catalyzing conversations among stakeholders on new approaches to understanding and meeting these challenges.

B

Workshop Agenda

TUESDAY, NOVEMBER 12, 2024

8:30–9:00 Welcome and Opening Remarks

Kasia Kornecki, National Academies of Sciences, Engineering, and Medicine's Board on Energy and Environmental Systems
Benjamin Lee, University of Pennsylvania, Planning Committee Chair

9:00–9:30 Keynote Presentation—Evolution of Data Center Energy Use

Lawrence Berkeley National Laboratory (LBNL) has studied and modeled the growth of data center energy use for more than 25 years. Dr. Arman Shehabi (LBNL) will describe how data center energy use has evolved over the past two decades, sometimes rapidly increasing and at other times remaining relatively flat and discuss the drivers of that change. Dr. Shehabi will also present findings from the upcoming 2024 Data Center Energy Report to Congress and how the rise of highly specialized hardware and artificial intelligence are changing the data center landscape and creating new opportunities for efficiency and decarbonization. A Q&A session with the audience will follow.

9:40–11:00 Moderated Panel Discussion—AI Technologies: Trends and Future Use Cases

This session will examine the trajectory of artificial intelligence, taking a holistic view of data processing, training, and inference. Opening remarks will elevate emerging models and applications driving future computational demands. The following moderated discussion will explore the implications of future use cases on electricity use and computing resource demands.

Moderator: Benjamin Lee, University of Pennsylvania, Planning Committee Chair
Speakers:
- Eric Xing, Carnegie Mellon University
- Prakhar Mehrotra, Blackstone

11:10–12:40 Moderated Panel Discussion—Data Center Infrastructure

This session will examine how data center design and operations adapt—and should continue to evolve—to meet the rising energy demands of artificial intelligence workloads. Opening remarks will explore how data centers can achieve greater flexibility in their power consumption. A moderated panel discussion will focus on coupling flexible computing and infrastructure management, including cooling, with realistic performance and sustainability goals, ensuring scalability and responsiveness in the face of AI-driven demand.

Moderator: Ayse Coskun, Boston University, Planning Committee Member
Speakers:
- Adam Wierman, California Institute of Technology and Verrus
- Andrew Chien, University of Chicago
- Peter de Bock, Department of Energy, Advanced Research Projects Agency–Energy
- Ricardo Bianchini, Microsoft (Azure)

1:00–1:30 Fireside Chat—System Operator Perspectives on Connecting Grid-Friendly Data Centers

This session will highlight the on-the-ground experiences of utilities as more data centers are connected to the grid.

Representatives from the Electric Reliability Council of Texas and Virginia's Dominion Energy will highlight the challenges and opportunities they are seeing in their states.

Moderator: K. John Holmes, National Academies' Board on Energy and Environmental Systems
Speakers:
- Agee Springer, Electric Reliability Council of Texas
- Robert Wright, Dominion Energy

1:40–2:10 Keynote Presentation—Impact of Data Centers: Projected Power Use and Potential Implications for the Grid

Dr. Thomas Wilson (Electric Power Research Institute) will discuss projections of power use by U.S. data centers, requests for data center connections, and potential implications for the grid. The keynote presentation will also highlight the possibilities for more flexible data center operations to accelerate artificial intelligence development while minimizing costs, lowering carbon emissions, and enhancing system reliability. A Q&A session with the audience will follow.

2:20–3:50 Moderated Panel Discussion—Impact of Data Centers on the Grid

This session will examine the increasing impact of large data centers on the electric power grid. A moderated discussion will elevate recommendations for how to handle load growth from data centers and maintain grid reliability.

Moderator: Thomas Wilson, Electric Power Research Institute
Speakers:
- Bruce Tsuchida, Brattle
- Costa Samaras, Carnegie Mellon University
- Line Roald, University of Wisconsin–Madison
- Ravi Jain, Tapestry (Google)

4:00–5:40 Moderated Panel Discussion—Sustainability Analysis of Data Centers

This session will discuss the sustainability impacts of data centers, including their environmental and human dimensions. Opening remarks will explore current data, methods, and standards, as well as gaps and hurdles, in analyzing energy, climate, water, waste, and community impacts of data centers from a life-cycle perspective. A moderated panel discussion will highlight potential solutions for addressing these gaps and identify areas that need further research.

Moderator: Eric Masanet, University of California, Santa Barbara, Planning Committee Member
Speakers:

- Cooper Elsworth, Google
- Davide D'Ambrosio, International Energy Agency
- Julie Bolthouse, Piedmont Environmental Council
- Laura Gonzalez Guerrero, Clean Virginia
- Sarah Boyd, Aligned Incentives

WEDNESDAY, NOVEMBER 13, 2024

9:00–9:05 Welcome and Opening Remarks

9:05–9:35 Keynote Presentation—Efficiency Through Technology Advancement: Hardware–Software Interactions

Modern large language models (LLMs) have generated tremendous value and productivity improvements across almost all areas of human endeavor and, as a result, demand for both training and inference is growing at exponential rates which in turn drives a huge demand for energy. Over the last decade, numerous hardware improvements have improved the energy efficiency of LLM inference by 1000x. Similar gains have been made on the software (model) side. Dr. William Dally (NVIDIA) will describe the major contributors to this efficiency gain and the expected trend in hardware and model efficiency. A Q&A session with the audience will follow.

9:45–11:15 Moderated Panel Discussion—Efficiency Through Technology Advancement: Hardware–Software Interactions

This session will examine opportunities to improve carbon efficiency and sustainability through the coordinated design of hardware and software. Opening remarks will define the landscape of hardware platforms and the role of specialized architectures for artificial intelligence. A moderated panel discussion will explore the software strategies required to achieve high performance and efficiency on these architectures.

Moderator: Carole-Jean Wu, Meta, Planning Committee Member
Speakers:
- Miloš Popovic, Ayar Labs
- Tamar Eilam, International Business Machines Corporation
- Valerie Taylor, Argonne National Laboratory
- Vivienne Sze, Massachusetts Institute of Technology
- William Dally, NVIDIA

11:25–12:55 Moderated Panel Discussion—Societal Considerations of Data Center Expansion

This session will consider the impact of data center expansion on local economies and communities. A moderated panel discussion will highlight concerns related to local energy consumption, environmental impact, and workforce, weighing these aspects alongside the potential benefits of growth in artificial intelligence.

Moderator: Prashant Shenoy, University of Massachusetts Amherst, Planning Committee Member
Speakers:
- Kelly Sanders, University of Southern California
- Nate Benforado, Southern Environmental Law Center
- Tim Cywinski, Sierra Club
- Varun Rai, University of Texas at Austin

1:00–2:00 Closing Remarks
This concluding session will take a forward-looking perspective on artificial intelligence and data centers. Each planning committee member will discuss their perspective on the challenges discussed through the workshop and the role of industry, academic research, and policy makers in contributing to the solution space.

Speakers:
- Benjamin Lee, University of Pennsylvania, Planning Committee Chair
- Ayse Coskun, Boston University
- Eric Masanet, University of California, Santa Barbara
- Prashant Shenoy, University of Massachusetts Amherst
- Carole-Jean Wu, Meta

C

Planning Committee and Speaker Biographical Information

PLANNING COMMITTEE

BENJAMIN C. LEE, *Chair*, is a professor of electrical and systems engineering and computer and information science at the University of Pennsylvania. He is also a visiting researcher at Google in the Global Infrastructure Group. Dr. Lee's research focuses on computer architecture (microprocessors, memories, data centers), energy efficiency, environmental sustainability, and security. He builds interdisciplinary links to machine learning and algorithmic game theory to better design and manage computer systems. His research on environmentally sustainable computing, in collaboration with Harvard University, received an Expedition in Computing award from the National Science Foundation (NSF) in 2024. Dr. Lee was an assistant and then associate professor at Duke University. He received his postdoctorate in electrical engineering at Stanford University, PhD in computer science from Harvard University, and BS in electrical engineering and computer science from the University of California (UC), Berkeley. He has also held visiting positions at Meta AI, Microsoft Research, Intel Labs, and Lawrence Livermore National Laboratory. Dr. Lee received the NSF Computing Innovation Fellowship, NSF CAREER Award, and Google Faculty Research Award. He is an Institute of Electrical and Electronics Engineers (IEEE) fellow and Association for Computing Machinery (ACM) distinguished scientist.

AYSE K. COSKUN is a full professor at Boston University (BU) in the Department of Electrical and Computer Engineering, where she leads the Performance and Energy Aware Computing Laboratory (PeacLab) to solve problems toward making computer systems more intelligent and energy efficient. Dr. Coskun is also the director of the BU Center for Information and Systems Engineering (CISE) and recently served as the interim associate dean for research at the BU College of Engineering. Her research interests intersect design automation, computer systems, and architecture. Her research outcomes are culminated in several technical awards, including the NSF CAREER Award, the IEEE CEDA Ernest Kuh Early Career Award, and an IBM Faculty Award. Dr. Coskun is a senior member of IEEE and ACM, and she currently serves as the deputy editor-in-chief of the *IEEE Transactions on Computer Aided Design*. She received her PhD in computer engineering from UC San Diego.

BENJAMIN KROPOSKI is the director of the Power Systems Engineering Center at the National Renewable Energy Laboratory (NREL) where he leads NREL's strategic research in the design, planning, and operations of electrical power systems. He has more than 30 years of experience in the design, testing, and integration of renewable and distributed power systems. As an IEEE fellow, Dr. Kroposki was recognized for his leadership in renewable and distributed energy systems integration. He received his BSEE and MSEE from Virginia Tech and PhD from the Colorado School of Mines. Dr. Kroposki is also an adjunct professor at the Colorado School of Mines and the University of Colorado and teaches courses on integrating renewable energy into power systems. He serves as the organizational director for the Universal Interoperability for Grid-Forming Inverters Consortium tackling the challenges with seamless integration of inverter-based resources and synchronous machines in all power systems.

ERIC MASANET is the Mellichamp Chair in Sustainability Science for Emerging Technologies at UC Santa Barbara, where he is also a professor in the Bren School of Environmental Science and Management and (by courtesy) in the Department of Mechanical Engineering. He has co-authored more than 150 scientific publications on sustainability modeling of energy and materials demand systems, with particular focuses on data centers and information technology (IT) systems. He has held numerous service roles to help advance energy and climate technology policy and their scientific evidence bases. These include service as the head of the Energy Demand Technology Unit at the International Energy Agency in Paris (2015–2017), a lead author of the Intergovernmental Panel on Climate Change's (IPCC's) Sixth Assessment Report (Chapter 5: Demand), an author of the Fifth U.S. National Climate Assessment, a member of the research advisory board of the American Council for an Energy Efficient Economy (2019–2024), and as a consultant at the U.S. White House

Office of Science and Technology Policy (2022–2024). He holds a PhD in mechanical engineering, with an emphasis on sustainable design and manufacturing, from UC Berkeley.

PRASHANT SHENOY is currently a distinguished professor and associate dean in the College of Information and Computer Sciences at the University of Massachusetts Amherst. His research interests lie in distributed systems and networking, with a recent emphasis on cloud and sustainable computing. He has been the recipient of several best paper awards at leading conferences, including a Sigmetrics Test of Time Award. He serves on the editorial boards of several journals and has served as the program chair of more than a dozen ACM and IEEE conferences. He is a fellow of ACM, IEEE, the American Association for the Advancement of Science (AAAS), and the American Institute of Aeronautics and Astronautics (AIAA). He received the BTech degree in computer science and engineering from the Indian Institute of Technology, Bombay, and an MS and a PhD in computer science from the University of Texas at Austin (UT Austin).

CAROLE-JEAN WU is a director of artificial intelligence (AI) research at Meta, where she leads the Systems and Machine Learning Research team. She is a founding member and a vice president of MLCommons, a nonprofit organization that aims to accelerate machine learning innovations for the benefit of all. Prior to Meta/Facebook, Dr. Wu was a tenured professor at Arizona State University. Dr. Wu's expertise sits at the intersection of computer systems and machine learning, with a focus on performance, energy efficiency, and sustainability. Her work spans across data center infrastructures and edge systems. Dr. Wu's work has been recognized with several awards, including IEEE Micro Top Picks and ACM/IEEE Best Paper Awards. She is the recipient of the NSF CAREER Award, CRA-WP Anita Borg Early Career Award Distinction of Honorable Mention, IEEE Young Engineer of the Year Award, and Science Foundation Arizona Bisgrove Early Career Scholarship and is in the Hall of Fame of ACM/IEEE International Symposium on Computer Architecture, IEEE International Symposium on High-Performance Computer Architecture, and IEEE International Symposium on Workload Characterization. She earned her MA and PhD from Princeton University and BSc from Cornell University.

SPEAKERS

NATE BENFORADO is a senior attorney at the Southern Environmental Law Center. Based in Charlottesville, Virginia, his work focuses on energy and utility issues in Virginia—from reducing carbon dioxide emissions from power plants to advancing energy efficiency programs that lower energy bills and cut emissions. Data centers have been a significant issue in Virginia for years, but recent growth projections have elevated the issue even more. Mr. Benforado litigates cases at Virginia's State Corporation Commission, which regulates the state's utilities, and works on related legislation at the General Assembly.

RICARDO BIANCHINI is a technical fellow and the corporate vice president at Microsoft Azure, where he leads the team responsible for managing Azure's Compute workload, server capacity, and data center infrastructure with a strong focus on efficiency and sustainability. Before joining Azure in 2022, Dr. Bianchini led the Systems Research Group and the Cloud Efficiency team at Microsoft Research (MSR). During his tenure at MSR, he created research projects in power efficiency and intelligent resource management that resulted in large-scale production systems across Microsoft. Prior to joining Microsoft in 2014, Dr. Bianchini was a professor at Rutgers University, where he conducted research in data center power and energy management, energy-aware storage systems, energy-aware load distribution across data centers, and leveraging renewable energy in data centers. He received his PhD in computer science from the University of Rochester. He is a fellow of both ACM and IEEE.

JULIE BOLTHOUSE is the director of land use at Piedmont Environmental Council where she has worked for 14 years. She manages eight field staff that work on land use issues in Clarke, Loudoun, Fauquier, Rappahannock, Culpeper, Orange, Madison, Greene, and Albemarle counties. She holds a bachelor's degree in fisheries science with a minor in watershed management and two master's degrees in urban affairs and planning and natural resources. Her advocacy work has allowed her to work on a wide variety of land use issues for the past decade but for the past 3 years she has been focused primarily on the pressing issue of the growing data center market in Virginia and massive expansions of the state's energy infrastructure to serve it.

SARAH BOYD has spent her career using life-cycle assessment (LCA) to drive decision-making in the corporate world. She is the chief strategy officer of Aligned Incentives (now a part of Bureau Veritas) where she uses LCA at scale to identify granular carbon mitigation actions at the product and corporate level. Prior to joining Aligned Incentives, Dr. Boyd led product carbon footprinting for new product introductions at Apple. In her previous work in consulting, she led more than 100 product and corporate sustainability projects with clients across information and communication technology (ICT), electrical utilities, aerospace, construction, and consumer products sectors, and led data updates for the GaBi U.S. LCA database for Sphera. Dr. Boyd holds a BS from Stanford University and MS and PhD in mechanical engineering from UC Berkeley. Her book *Life-Cycle Assessment of Semiconductors* has found broad use with sustainability practitioners in ICT looking to drive LCA-based decisions themselves.

ANDREW A. CHIEN is the William Eckhardt Distinguished Service Professor of Computer Science at the University of Chicago and senior scientist at Argonne National Laboratory. He has led the Zero-Carbon Cloud project since 2015 and is well known for his research on data centers, renewable energy and sustainability, cloud resource management and software, large-scale system architecture, and graph computing architecture. He is leader of the Intelligence Advanced Research Projects Activity–funded UpDown System Project, designing breakthrough scalable graph analytics systems. He is a leader in the NSF Expedition on Computational Decarbonization. Dr. Chien has received numerous recognitions for his research. He currently serves on the NSF CISE Advisory Committee, NSF Advisory Committee on Advanced Cyberinfrastructure, and the Defense Advanced Research Projects Agency (DARPA) Information Sciences and Technology (ISAT) advisory group. He is a fellow of ACM, IEEE, and AAAS. He served as the editor-in-chief of *Communications of the ACM* (2017–2022) and vice president of research at Intel Corporation (2005–2010). He has served on the faculty of the University of Illinois and as the SAIC Chair Professor at UC San Diego. He received his BS, MS, and PhD from the Massachusetts Institute of Technology (MIT).

TIM CYWINSKI is a political communications specialist who advocates for a livable, just future. His career in political, legislative, and social advocacy spans more than 14 years and has centered on pushing for policy that advances justice in the context of poverty, student rights, education, college affordability, economic security, sustainability, and climate change. Mr. Cywinski currently leads public relations and communications strategy at the Sierra Club Virginia Chapter with a focus on promoting environmental justice policy at the local, state, and federal levels. Prior to the Sierra Club, he held a multitude of positions related to electoral campaigning, community organizing, and federal and state level lobbying. Outside of his professional position, Mr. Cywinski presents strategic communications, grassroots planning, and legislative advocacy training to civic and community groups. He earned a bachelor's degree in political science from Roanoke College in 2015 and a master's degree in political communications and public relations and media from Johns Hopkins University in 2023.

WILLIAM DALLY joined NVIDIA in January 2009 as the chief scientist, after spending 12 years at Stanford University, where he was chair of the Computer Science Department. Dr. Dally and his Stanford team developed the system architecture, network architecture, signaling, routing, and synchronization technology that is found in most large parallel computers today. He was previously at MIT from 1986 to 1997, where he and his team built the J-Machine and the M-Machine, experimental parallel computer systems that pioneered the separation of mechanism from programming models and demonstrated very low overhead synchronization and communication mechanisms. From 1983 to 1986, he was at the California Institute of Technology (Caltech), where he designed the MOSSIM Simulation Engine and the Torus Routing chip, which pioneered "wormhole" routing and virtual-channel flow control. He is a member of the National Academy of Engineering, a fellow of the American Academy of Arts and Sciences, a fellow of IEEE and ACM, and has received the ACM Eckert-Mauchly Award, the IEEE Seymour Cray Award, and the ACM Maurice Wilkes award. He has published more than 250 papers, holds more than 120 issued patents, and is an author of four textbooks. Dr. Dally received a bachelor's degree in electrical engineering from Virginia Tech, a master's degree in electrical engineering from Stanford University, and a PhD in computer science from Caltech. He was a co-founder of Velio Communications and Stream Processors.

DAVIDE D'AMBROSIO is one of the lead authors of the World Energy Outlook (WEO) series and WEO special reports. Mr. D'Ambrosio's work includes extensive modeling and analysis to assess the long-term implications of current energy trends, government policies, and climate commitments. He is also the head of the Sustainability, Technology, and Outlooks Data Working Group at the International Energy Agency (IEA). He leads the development of data analytics and visualization tools for IEA's modeling teams, with a particular emphasis on policy and technology. Before joining the WEO team, he held various roles at IEA, working on energy statistics and energy technology. He holds a master's degree in computer science engineering.

PETER DE BOCK currently serves as the program director at the Advanced Research Projects Agency–Energy (ARPA-E) for the Department of Energy (DOE). At ARPA-E, Dr. de Bock leads and developed the ASCEND and PRE-TRAILS programs to realize a future of sustainable aviation. In addition, he developed the COOLERCHIPS program focused on making a transformational leap in efficiency of cooling of data centers and manages projects in the areas of ultra-high power density battery systems, hydrogen storage and propulsion, additive manufacturing, and power electronics. Prior to joining ARPA-E, Dr. de Bock worked at GE Research as a principal engineer for ThermoSciences and platform lead for Power-Thermal Mechanical Systems. He is the former chair of the ASME K-16 committee on heat transfer in electronics equipment, an ASME fellow, an AIAA member, and he holds more than 50 patents and publications. Dr. de Bock received his PhD in mechanical engineering from the University of Cincinnati and holds MSc degrees from the University of Twente in the Netherlands and the University of Warwick in the United Kingdom.

TAMAR EILAM is an IBM fellow and the chief scientist for sustainable computing in the IBM T.J. Watson Research Center in New York. Dr. Eilam is leading research aiming at drastically reducing the carbon footprint associated with computing across infrastructure, systems, and software, data, and AI. She completed a PhD in computer science in the Technion, Israel, in 2000. She joined the IBM T.J. Watson Research Center in New York as a research staff member that same year. She was recognized as an IBM fellow in 2014.

COOPER ELSWORTH is a researcher and corporate sustainability practitioner developing actionable emissions data to drive corporate decarbonization. He is a technical program manager at Google, where he manages data pipelines to monitor and reduce the emissions of Google's data center workloads, including those for AI products. These data power detailed emissions allocation and reporting to customers across Google's enterprise products. Dr. Elsworth previously advised Fortune 500 companies to advance their sustainability programs and developed sustainability software products at Watershed—a carbon accounting software startup. He also built near-real-time deforestation and forest carbon monitoring tools to enable agricultural commodity teams to reduce deforestation happening in their supply chains at Descartes Labs—a satellite imagery analytics startup. Prior to his work on corporate climate action, Dr. Elsworth's academic research identified ice sheet tipping points to better constrain sea-level rise. He holds a PhD in geophysics and an MS in computational mathematics from Stanford University and an MS and a BS in engineering science from Pennsylvania State University.

LAURA GONZALEZ GUERRERO is currently working as an energy and regulatory policy manager at Clean Virginia since October 2020. Her master's degree is in public policy from the University of Virginia. She was part of the DOE summer internship program, where she worked on fuel cells and hydrogen technologies implementation. For her graduation project, Ms. Guerrero worked with the Energy Office of South Carolina, studying options to increase access to clean energy for low- to moderate-income communities. She has previously worked in net-neutrality policy and online privacy topics in Colombia.

RAVI JAIN is the head of products and technology at Tapestry, the moonshot for applying AI to decarbonizing the electric grid at X (formerly Google X). Dr. Jain has held several roles developing groundbreaking technological products, including leading AI for augmented reality (AR) and Metaverse at Meta and Search AI and Alexa at Amazon. He also served as the chief technology officer for Microsoft co-founder Paul Allen's Vulcan Inc., a director for mobile advertising at Google, and a senior scientist at Bellcore. He has a PhD in computer science, more than 70 research papers, 3 books, and more than 30 patents. Dr. Jain is an IEEE fellow and an advisor to venture capital firms and startups.

PRAKHAR MEHROTRA is the managing director of applied AI at Blackstone. He is responsible for helping Blackstone's portfolio companies apply AI and capitalize on this powerful technology. Prior to joining Blackstone, Dr. Mehrotra served as the corporate vice president and head of applied AI for Walmart US. He led Walmart's team to win the prestigious Franz Edelman Prize 2023 by the Institute of Operations Research and Management Sciences (INFORMS) for its work on supply-chain optimization. Prior to Walmart, he led the AI group at Uber. He started his career as a data scientist at Twitter. Dr. Mehrotra holds a PhD in aeronautics from Caltech and a master's degree from École Polytechnique, Paris. He is a two-time recipient of the Edelman Medal (2020, 2023) and an IEEE senior member. He serves on the peer-review committee for major AI conferences (International Conference on Learning Representations, International Conference on Autonomous Agents and Multiagent Systems, Computer Vision and Pattern Recognition, INFORMS). He was named in the AI 100 list as top people in AI. During his graduate studies, he was awarded the Ernest E. Sechler Award in aeronautics by Caltech and the Gaspard Monge Medal from École Polytechnique.

MILOŠ POPOVIC is a senior technical architect and the co-founder at Ayar Labs, a technology startup developing optical input/output (I/O) chiplets, based on silicon photonics, to enable the efficient scaling of AI and other computer hardware via optical interconnection. The technology stemmed from early research and demonstrations in his and his collaborators' university research groups, which included demonstration of the first microprocessor that communicates using light in 2015. Dr. Popovic is also an associate professor of electrical and computer engineering at BU and in the BU Photonics Center, where he leads the Silicon Photonics Research

Group. He received his BSc in electrical engineering from Queen's University, Canada, and his MS and PhD from MIT. Previously, he was on the faculty at the University of Colorado Boulder. His interests are in the theory and design of novel photonic integrated circuit technologies and in the on-chip integration of photonics and CMOS electronics. He is an author or co-author of more than 45 patents and 250 journal and conference papers. Dr. Popovic is a fellow of the Packard Foundation and of the National Academy of Inventors.

VARUN RAI is the Walt and Elspeth Rostow Professor in the LBJ School of Public Affairs at UT Austin, with a joint appointment in mechanical engineering. Through his interdisciplinary research at the interface of complex systems, decision science, and public policy, he studies emergence in socio-technical systems, with applications toward the design of a sustainable and resilient global energy system. He was a Global Economic Fellow in 2009 and a commissioner for the vertically integrated electric utility Austin Energy from 2013–2015. At UT Austin, he has served as the associate dean for research for the LBJ School (2017–2022) and as the director of the UT Austin Energy Institute (2019–2021). In 2016, the Association for Public Policy Analysis and Management awarded him the David N. Kershaw Award and Prize, which "was established to honor persons who, at under the age of 40, have made a distinguished contribution to the field of public policy analysis and management." He received his PhD and MS in mechanical engineering from Stanford University and a bachelor's degree in mechanical engineering from the Indian Institute of Technology, Kharagpur.

LINE ROALD is an associate professor in the Department of Electrical and Computer Engineering at University of Wisconsin–Madison, where she leads the Wisconsin Power Optimization research group focused on the optimization, sustainability, and resiliency of electric power grids. She received her PhD in electrical engineering (2016) from ETH Zurich, Switzerland, and was a postdoctoral research fellow at Los Alamos National Laboratory. She is the recipient of an NSF CAREER award, the Vilas Early Career Investigator Award, and several best paper awards and has co-authored more than 100 scientific papers. Her research interests center on the modeling and optimization of the electric grid—and infrastructures that depend on it—with a particular focus on managing uncertainty and risk from extreme weather and renewable energy variability.

COSTA SAMARAS is the director of Carnegie Mellon University's (CMU's) Scott Institute for Energy Innovation and the Trustee Professor of Civil and Environmental Engineering. He is an affiliated faculty member in the Department of Engineering and Public Policy and in the Heinz College of Information Systems and Public Policy. He analyzes how technologies and policies affect energy and emissions pathways, security, climate resilience, and economic and equity outcomes. From 2021–2024, he served in the White House Office of Science and Technology Policy (OSTP) as the principal assistant director for energy, OSTP chief advisor for energy policy, and then OSTP chief advisor for the clean energy transition. He assessed technologies and policies to achieve national climate commitments, co-led the White House report *U.S. Innovation to Meet 2050 Climate Goals,* co-led the climate and clean energy efforts of the President's Executive Order on Artificial Intelligence, and led the White House report on the climate and energy implications of digital assets. He was previously a senior researcher at the RAND Corporation as well as a megaprojects engineer in New York City. He received a joint PhD in civil and environmental engineering and engineering and public policy from CMU.

KELLY SANDERS is an associate professor in the University of Southern California's Sonny Astani Department of Civil and Environmental Engineering, currently on academic leave to serve as the assistant director of energy systems innovation at OSTP. Her research aims to accelerate the pace decarbonization and electrification, analyze tensions between climate change adaptation and mitigation strategies, and reduce the environmental impacts of providing energy and water. Dr. Sanders has authored more than 50 peer-reviewed publications and has been recognized in Forbes' 30 under 30 in energy, MIT Technology Review's 35 innovators under 35, and the American Academy of Environmental Engineers and Scientists 40 under 40 for her contributions to the energy field. In 2019, she was granted an NSF Early CAREER award. Her research and commentary have been featured in national and international media outlets, including *The New York Times, The Los Angeles Times, The Washington Post, Foreign Affairs, WIRED* magazine, *Forbes,* Bloomberg, *The Wall Street Journal,* and *Scientific American.* Dr. Sanders received her BS in bioengineering from Pennsylvania State University and an MSE and a PhD in mechanical engineering and environmental engineering from UT Austin.

ARMAN SHEHABI is a staff scientist in the Energy Analysis and Environmental Impacts Division of the Energy Technologies Area at Lawrence Berkeley National Laboratory (LBNL). He has more than 15 years of experience measuring and modeling the potential energy, economic, and air pollutant impacts associated with the large-scale adoption of clean energy policy and technologies for buildings and manufacturing, with extensive research focused on ICT. Dr. Shehabi's research at LBNL applies LCA methods to explore systems-wide energy, emissions, and materials flows through buildings and industrial sectors. His current work is focused on emerging technologies and industries in the areas of data center energy/water use, electronic waste recycling, building material circularity, and industrial decarbonization. Dr. Shehabi has authored more than 50 journal articles, research reports, and conference papers. His work has been published in *Science* magazine and *Nature* journals, cited in U.S. congressional legislation, and featured in BBC, NPR, and *New York Times* stories. Prior to joining LBNL, Dr. Shehabi held fellowship positions with the National Academy of Sciences in Washington, DC, and with the Consortium on Green Design and Manufacturing at UC Berkeley. He received his MS and PhD in environmental engineering from Stanford University and UC Berkeley, respectively, with an emphasis in building energy use and indoor air quality. Between graduate programs, he also worked as an engineering consultant and LEED-Accredited Professional to develop and implement sustainable building metrics.

AGEE SPRINGER is a senior manager of Grid Interconnections at the Electric Reliability Council of Texas (ERCOT). His department is responsible for the reliable integration of all generation and large load interconnection requests into the ERCOT system. Prior to assuming this position, Mr. Springer served as the manager of Large Load Integration, which oversees the interim interconnection process for large loads, develops ERCOT Protocol and Planning Guide revisions to ensure their reliable operation on the ERCOT system, and provides support for ERCOT's Large Flexible Load Task Force. His past experience at ERCOT includes developing situational awareness displays for the ERCOT control room, providing real-time engineering support and training for ERCOT system operators, performing analyses of ERCOT operational and market data, and leading ERCOT's Engineer Development Program. He has also served as the manager of market operations for RWE Renewables Americas. He holds a BS in physics from Duke University and an MSEE from UT Austin.

VIVIENNE SZE is a professor in the Department of Electrical Engineering and Computer Science at MIT. She works on computing systems that enable energy-efficient machine learning, computer vision, and video compression/processing for a wide range of applications, including autonomous navigation, digital health, and the Internet of Things.

VALERIE TAYLOR is the director of the Mathematics and Computer Science Division and a distinguished fellow at Argonne National Laboratory. Her research is in high-performance computing, with a focus on performance analysis, modeling, and tuning of parallel, scientific applications using AI. Her current work is on energy efficient methods. Prior to joining Argonne, she was the senior associate dean of academic affairs in the College of Engineering and a regents professor and the Royce E. Wisenbaker Professor in the Department of Computer Science and Engineering (CSE) at Texas A&M University. In 2003, she joined Texas A&M University as the department head of CSE, where she remained in that position until 2011. Prior to joining Texas A&M, Dr. Taylor was a member of the faculty in the Department of Electrical Engineering and Computer Science at Northwestern University for 11 years. She is also the chief executive officer and president of the Center for Minorities and People with Disabilities in IT, for which she is a co-founder. Dr. Taylor is a fellow of IEEE, ACM, and AAAS. She earned her BS in electrical and computer engineering and MS in computer engineering from Purdue University in 1985 and 1986, respectively, and PhD in electrical engineering and computer science from UC Berkeley in 1991.

T. BRUCE TSUCHIDA is a principal of The Brattle Group and has more than 30 years of experience in domestic and international power generation development, utility operations, and energy market analysis. He specializes in bridging technology, economics, and regulatory policy, particularly in assessing the impact of new technologies and regulatory changes. His expertise is largely in the electricity industry but also expands into the natural gas industry, includes integration studies for intermittent resources such as wind and solar power, storage technologies, operational logic studies, ancillary service studies, new load studies, and analyses required for regulatory proceedings. His work associated with regulatory proceedings includes cost-benefit analyses, such as evaluating new technologies and the resource portfolio, as well as cost of service studies and rate design. He has analyzed and modeled market restructuring for the energy industry and power systems and evaluated utility business model options associated with the change in markets (structural changes through deregulation or varying cost allocation methods, and landscape changes such as increase in renewables, change in fuel requirements, or evolving load types). Mr. Tsuchida holds two MS degrees from MIT, one in electrical engineering and computer science and the other in technology and policy. He holds a BE in mechanical engineering from Waseda University in Tokyo, Japan.

ADAM WIERMAN is the Carl F. Braun Professor in the Department of Computing and Mathematical Sciences at Caltech. He is also a founding advisor for Verrus, a startup building sustainable, grid-integrated data centers. He received his PhD, MSc, and BSc in computer science from CMU. Dr. Wierman's research strives to make the networked systems that govern our world sustainable and resilient. He is best known for his work spearheading the design of algorithms for sustainable data centers, which has seen significant industry adoption, and his work on heavy tails, including co-authoring the book *The Fundamentals of Heavy Tails*. He is a recipient of a variety of awards, including the ACM Sigmetrics Rising Star award, the ACM Sigmetrics Test of Time award, the IEEE INFOCOM Test of Time award, the IEEE Communications Society William R. Bennett Prize, the Caltech IDEA Advocate award, multiple teaching awards, and is a co-author of papers that have received "best paper" awards at a wide range of conferences across computer science, power engineering, and operations research.

THOMAS WILSON is a principal technical executive in the Integrated Grid and Energy Systems Division at the Electric Power Research Institute (EPRI). Dr. Wilson has conducted and managed research related to energy and environmental issues for more than 40 years, the majority of which he has spent at EPRI. He has served as a convening lead author for the U.S. National Climate Assessment and as a contributing author to IPCC's Fifth Assessment and has served in advisory roles to research groups, including MIT's Joint Program on the Science and Policy of Global Change, the University of Maryland's Global Energy Technology Strategy Program, Stanford University's Energy Modeling Forum, and NREL. From April 2022–June 2023, Dr. Wilson served as the assistant director for electricity at OSTP. He co-authored EPRI's white paper "Powering Intelligence: Analyzing Artificial Intelligence and Data Center Energy Consumption" and supported development of the Secretary of Energy Advisory Board recommendations to DOE on actions they could take to help power data centers.

ROBERT S. "ROBBIE" WRIGHT, JR., is the vice president, Strategic Partnerships, Dominion Energy Virginia. He leads the company's Strategic Partnerships team, which focuses on meeting the needs of the largest commercial, industrial, governmental, and electric wholesale customers for Dominion Energy Virginia. He also heads the Data Center Practice, Rural Broadband, and Energy Conservation organizations at Dominion Energy Virginia. Mr. Wright joined Dominion Energy in 1993 as an associate engineer and has held numerous technical, operational, and leadership roles related to the design, construction, and operation of the distribution system. In 2015, he was promoted to director of Electric Grid Planning and Asset Management at Dominion Energy Virginia, where he oversaw load planning and reliability performance for the electric distribution system, as well as vegetation management and asset data maintenance activities. Mr. Wright also has served as the lead witness for key areas of the company's Grid Transformation Plan filings since 2018. In 2022, he was named vice president for Grid and Technical Solutions for the company's Power Delivery Group. He assumed his current position in June 2024. He serves on the board of directors of the GridWise Alliance and is a member of the SEE Engineering and Operations Executive Committee. Mr. Wright received his bachelor's degree in electrical engineering from North Carolina State University. He is a Registered Professional Engineer in Virginia.

ERIC P. XING is the president of the Mohamed bin Zayed University of Artificial Intelligence, and a professor of computer science at CMU. He completed his undergraduate degree at Tsinghua University and holds a PhD in molecular biology and biochemistry from Rutgers University and a PhD in computer science from UC Berkeley. His main research interests are the development of machine learning and statistical methodology and large-scale distributed computational system and architectures for solving problems involving automated learning, reasoning, and decision-making in artificial, biological, and social systems. In recent years, he has been focusing on building large language models, world models, agent models, and foundation models for biology. Professor Xing has served on the editorial boards of leading scientific journals, including the *Journal of the American Statistical Association, Annals of Applied Statistics, PLOS Computational Biology*, and *Journal of Machine Learning Research*. He was a member of the DARPA ISAT advisory group, and a recipient of the NSF CAREER Award, Sloan Fellowship, Air Force Office of Scientific Research Young Investigator Award, IBM Open Collaborative Research Faculty Award, Carnegie Science Award, and best paper awards in several leading AI/computer science conferences such as the Association for Computational Linguistics, Neural Information Processing Systems, Operating Systems and Design Implementation, and Intelligent Systems for Molecular Biology. He is a fellow of the Association for the Advancement of Artificial Intelligence, ACM, the American Statistical Association, IEEE, and the Institute of Mathematical Statistics.